THE A–Z OF PRIMARY LEADERSHIP

CHRIS NOURSE-GREWAL

SERIES EDITOR: ROY BLATCHFORD

Together we unlock every learner's unique potential

At Hachette Learning (formerly Hodder Education), there's one thing we're certain about. No two students learn the same way. That's why our approach to teaching begins by recognising the needs of individuals first.

Our mission is to allow every learner to fulfil their unique potential by empowering those who teach them. From our expert teaching and learning resources to our digital educational tools that make learning easier and more accessible for all, we provide solutions designed to maximise the impact of learning for every teacher, parent and student.

Aligned to our parent company, Hachette Livre, founded in 1826, we pride ourselves on being a learning solutions provider with a global footprint.

www.hachettelearning.com

Although every effort has been made to ensure that website addresses are correct at time of going to press, Hachette Learning cannot be held responsible for the content of any website mentioned in this book. It is sometimes possible to find a relocated web page by typing in the address of the home page for a website in the URL window of your browser.

Hachette UK's policy is to use papers that are natural, renewable and recyclable products and made from wood grown in well-managed forests and other controlled sources. The logging and manufacturing processes are expected to conform to the environmental regulations of the country of origin.

To order, please visit www.hachettelearning.com or contact Customer Service at education@hachette.co.uk / +44 (0)1235 827827.

ISBN: 978 1 0360 0506 1

© Chris Nourse-Grewal 2025

First published in 2025 by
Hachette Learning (a trading division of Hodder & Stoughton Limited),
An Hachette UK Company
Carmelite House
50 Victoria Embankment
London EC4Y 0DZ
www.hachettelearning.com

The authorised representative in the EEA is Hachette Ireland, 8 Castlecourt Centre, Dublin 15, D15 XTP3, Ireland (email: info@hbgi.ie)

Impression number 10 9 8 7 6 5 4 3 2 1
Year   2029 2028 2027 2026 2025

All rights reserved. Apart from any use permitted under UK copyright law, no part of this publication may be reproduced or transmitted in any form or by any means, electronic or mechanical, including photocopying and recording, or held within any information storage and retrieval system, without permission in writing from the publisher or under licence from the Copyright Licensing Agency Limited. Further details of such licences (for reprographic reproduction) may be obtained from the Copyright Licensing Agency Limited, www.cla.co.uk

Typeset in the UK.
Printed and bound by CPI Group (UK) Ltd, Croydon, CR0 4YY

A catalogue record for this title is available from the British Library.

CONTENTS

Dedication v
About the author vi
Acknowledgements viii
Foreword by Roy Blatchford ix

Section One

Assemble 3
Behaviour 9
Children 15
Delegation 21
Empathy 29
Free school meals 37
Governance 45
Holistic 51
Inspection 57
Journey 65
Kindness 71
Leadership 75
Money 81
Noise 87
Outstanding 93
Performance 99
Questioning 107

Revolution 113

Self-regulation 121

Teaching 129

Understanding 137

Vision 145

Wayne 151

Xenial 157

Yourself 163

Zillions 169

Section Two

1. The five keys to a successful school 177

2. Teaching and learning Continua 179

3. The KBZA character curriculum 181

4. In-class behaviour flow chart for students 185

5. Oracy – why? 187

6. Middle leaders – pupil progress proforma 189

7. Holistic development – balancing the whole child 193

8. AI policy points for governance 195

9. The ripple effect 197

References 198

*I dedicate this book to the memory of my nephew, Joshan Carr.
A kind, passionate, energetic and funny young man who was
everyone's best friend and generous with both his time and his heart.*

25th January 2004 – 21st March 2025

ABOUT THE AUTHOR

Chris Nourse-Grewal is a lifer. He started his journey into education at 18 with a BEd (Hons) in primary education, and has continued to teach, lead and develop schools ever since. From cutting his teeth in a well-run primary school in Chelmsford to the challenge of teaching and leading in two inner London primary schools, Chris has seen how schools can thrive or not due to the quality and imagination of school leaders.

His first headship was in a junior school in Southampton, followed by an amalgamation of an infant and junior into a primary school in Surrey, while opening a new children's centre and a special needs base.

An international opportunity led Chris to become the founding principal of a new primary school in Abu Dhabi in the United Arab Emirates (UAE) followed by a brief stint as a director of educational strategy. A return to Blighty to run a large primary school in Dorset was short-lived, and Chris returned to the UAE to be the principal of an all-age British curriculum school, which he grew from the early years foundation stage to Year 13. His three children attended his school for nine years.

As an executive principal and trained inspector, Chris then moved into school improvement and supported a group of schools with teaching and learning, raising expectations and growing a positive school culture among other things. He has jumped into temporary headship to move schools out of trouble, managing US New England Association of Schools and Colleges curriculum accreditation at the same time.

Chris is currently the executive principal of Khalifa Bin Zayed Al Awal (KBZA) School in Abu Dhabi, a pilot school for the UAE government to trial different approaches to public education – a mix of British rigour and International Baccalaureate learning frameworks are proving very successful, as has been bringing the children's centre approach to the school.

Chris enjoys music and can often be found in guitar shops wondering how he could possibly justify to his wife that buying another guitar would be a wise investment!

ACKNOWLEDGEMENTS

In writing this *A–Z of Primary Leadership*, I must acknowledge those who have shaped my experience of leading over the past 25 years of headship. My first headteacher, as an NQT, was Peter Terry in Essex. He taught me valuable lessons about being on the school gate, listening to parents and children, and authentically caring about the children and teachers.

In London schools I learned about resilience and the power of humour in the staffroom. In Walthamstow, I learned to survive from Linda Bennet – strict, no-nonsense but warm and compassionate. In Wandsworth, I saw unhappiness and disillusionment in the eyes of my colleges, and I learned from that too.

In Southampton, I learned that a caretaker could be king – and Ralph Payne was as supportive and kind to the staff and children as it is possible to be: sugary tea sitting in his tool shed was worth a thousand hours of therapy. And, of course, the real boss of any primary school – our wonderful office managers Sheila Craft and Leanne Taylor, who found budgets to improve things from thin air and ran the parent-teacher association with aplomb.

In Surrey, I learned about the power of children's centre goodness for a community and how a specialist provision could be truly integrated.

The great teachers I learned from are too many to name; the school governors and parents who put their faith in me to lead their schools, thank you.

FOREWORD

Primary schools are good places to be. I have visited many hundreds over the past few years, at home and abroad. What do I see typically at the beating heart of primary education?

- Leaders' infectious style which enables staff to be creative and seize opportunities to shape innovative, exciting and fun learning opportunities within and beyond the classroom.
- A strong work and team ethic among teachers and support staff.
- Positive relationships between staff and children, working in harmonious multicultural communities.
- Abundant, up-to-date, attractive resources which motivate children to learn and develop enquiring minds.
- Fit-for-purpose systems for keeping children safe and tracking their progress; children's self-esteem is high.

These five aspects and so much more. And in the very best of primary schools, you walk away thinking 'someone's doing something special there'.

Research and observations inform educationalists that excellence is a habit in so many primary schools today. In turn, parents report high degrees of satisfaction with what their children experience day by day. For those 'children on the margins', one sees everywhere teachers and support staff going the extra mile to ensure a climate of inclusion.

What we know about effective schools is that success doesn't happen by chance. Confident leaders plan carefully, take colleagues with them, keep children at the heart of their visions, and deliver with ambition and a fine eye for detail.

Thus, the best classrooms and corridors manifest high expectations and high all-round standards; excellent displays of children's work; pupils studying independently and collaboratively; pupils speaking confidently about their subjects and making meaningful connections between topics; and exercise books, portfolios and online files that demonstrate vibrant curriculum progression.

Wise leaders know equally well that there can be bumps in the road and occasional crises. They deal with the triumphs and disasters with equanimity, rooted in their own experiences and values. They balance skilfully the individual therapeutic needs of the individual with the greater good. They communicate openly and genuinely.

Further, as this author admirably shows, effective leadership requires humility, kindness and a well-judged sense of humour. High quality storytelling is integral to the primary leader's personal and professional playbook.

***

In common with other titles in this A–Z series, section one is orchestrated around the 26 letters of the English alphabet. Section two offers a range of curriculum models and contemporary materials for the primary leader.

Chris Nourse-Grewal takes the reader on an authoritative and affectionate journey from Assemble and Empathy, through Money and Revolution, to Wayne and Yourself. He is a school leader of significant experience in the UK and internationally. His talking-the-walk and walking-the-talk approach radiates in every chapter.

Roy Blatchford, series editor

SECTION ONE

ASSEMBLE

Assemble: 'gather together in one place for a common purpose'.

Oxford English Dictionary

Do you remember that teacher? You know – the one that made you feel special and motivated to learn? Perhaps you shared a sense of humour with them, or a love of the subject, or perhaps they were just kind and supportive.

During staff meetings headteachers occasionally reflect with their staff on why we are all here. Often, the discussion will move to why we all became teachers – what attracted us to the profession. It is never the holidays or the pay. Some leaders will tell stories from their own life about the good, the bad and the ugly of the teaching profession and the impact, both positive and negative, that this had on them as learners.

Movingly, staff share that it was a special teacher who saw ability where others had overlooked them; a teacher or a coach who had encouraged a passion for sport or music, for example, which had led to their career choices. For others, the vehicle of fiction had lit fires of fascination for education that would only be satisfied by entering into the profession. The film *Dead Poets Society* (Weir, 1989) has been named – with its message of *carpe diem* or 'seize the day' – as a reason why some people were delightfully ensnared by teaching.

'The great play goes on,' Mr Keating says to his students in *Dead Poets Society*, 'and you may contribute a verse – what will your verse be?' What a privilege to be alongside learners as they start to assemble ideas, passions and interests which will shape their lives.

In leadership you assemble your senior leadership team and middle leadership team, your teaching staff, teaching assistants, administrative staff, support staff and governing body. As the headteacher you are the centre of gravity of your learning community. You are the conductor of multiple stakeholder groups simultaneously: parents' council, 'helping hands' groups (hearing children read), student council, local education authority colleagues, multi-academy trust teams and other community groups, especially if you are a faith school.

How effectively (and routinely) you are able to stand before these different groups with their differing expectations and agendas – sticking firmly to your beliefs and principles – will determine your success. Diplomacy and patience are, of course, required to better understand the needs of your learning community, but also the ability to convey in a few words your core beliefs, such as inclusion, equal opportunities and high expectations for all as the non-negotiables.

SENIOR LEADERSHIP TEAM

Getting the right balance in your senior team is crucial. A good starting point is to reflect on what kind of leader you are? Are you the visionary running off into the distance hoping that the team can keep up; or are you the details person, pragmatic and grounded; maybe you are the data person entrenched in key performance indicators; or maybe you are the empath listening carefully to the ebb and flow of the staff, students and parents.

Whichever one you are, and be brutally honest here, make sure you build a team of complementary skills around you.

A common error is to recruit clones of yourself, which makes for comfortable meetings with easy alignment; however, leaders soon realise they are missing key skill sets. If, in fact, you tend to be the big-picture thinker, visionary, what could and should our school look like kind of person, but you are less good on the detail, then recruit people who are meticulous in their thinking and planning. In that way, with a 'whole brain team' approach, leadership teams are able to improve their schools rapidly, as together they have most bases covered.

If you are in a small school, you will be wearing many hats at once. This is a huge challenge – for example, acting caretaker and deputy head,

SENCo, health and safety officer, early career teacher (ECT) mentor – the list goes on. Hats off to those small schools; my experience is to network widely with other schools so that you can share ideas, resources and maybe even teachers, administrators and teaching assistants.

ASSEMBLY

Many readers will recall that the summit of an outstanding assembly, as judged by the government inspector, was the presence and power of 'awe and wonder'.

Many school leaders were confused as to how they could conjure up these two genies from the assembly that would usually contain 'Autumn Days', sung and/or mimed by a well-meaning but not so tuneful hall of youngsters. If you were lucky this was followed by an enthusiastic young teacher, who was also the eco-club leader, showcasing global warming through interpretive dance, much to the glee of the more seasoned teachers at the back of the hall.

In some cases, it was fairly awful, and we wondered when it would stop. It may be an apocryphal story, but one colleague told me that during their school inspection they received 'outstanding' for awe and wonder. She went on to tell me that the inspectors were glowing about the children's views that they always knew they would see awe and wonder in the assembly. Little did the inspectors know that 'Awe and Wonder' were the names of the two goldfish who had a home on top of the stereo equipment in the hall.

On a more serious note, the assembly is one of your main communication/marketing opportunities for children, teachers and parents. A bit of stand-up for the headteacher to both wow and inspire the onlookers. A place for vision, values and expectations to be shared and celebrated. The use of music, dance, drama and a formal presentation that brings the fun and fundamentals of primary learning alive. For parents, it is a time to be proud of their children and their achievements.

Well-orchestrated assemblies can be funny, emotional, inspiring, uplifting and bring cohesion to your learning community. They can develop a culture of pride in the school that radiates out into the community and the WhatsApp groups.

Success starts to breed success – parents become more interested in your curriculum evenings because their children are leading them. Community BBQs and parent–teacher association (PTA) fairs bring people together with a common purpose of supporting *our* children in *our* school. The notion of the identity of the school grows in the community, and people start to be more willing to identify with it – pupils more willing to attend each and every day of the school year.

The assembly then is the shop window of your school, elements of which you can open to the wider community through social media. Nothing has more positive power for a school than a child proudly sharing what they have learned in front of their learning community in a high quality and well-produced assembly.

Put simply it is 'Achieving Together' in action, a motto that resonates in many schools. This strategic intention of all being able to achieve is powerful: students and teachers, students and students, teachers and parents achieving together.

CODA

When we assemble, when we gather together in one place for a common purpose we can achieve great things. What are the key ingredients?

- Assemble a 'whole brain team'.
- Remind the team why they became educators and the consequences of poor schooling.
- 'Awe and wonder' – make assemblies uplifting, fun, relevant, surprising, student led and involve the wider community.
- Use assemblies to send a message of the school's intent to the wider learning community: This is what we stand for and who we are – support us!
- Celebrate authentic achievements – from teachers running a 10K race, to a student's black belt in karate, to 50 house points, to the caretaker who has completed 10 years' service at the school.
- Involve your governors in assemblies as they often hear only the bad news stories.
- Success breeds success. Make success a habit – make assembly sing!

ASIDE

SINGING ASSEMBLY

There is undeniably something special about community singing when it's done well, as it brings a school together, literally singing from the same sheet.

The benches are out at the back of the hall for Year 6, the projector has the words ready and if you're lucky Ms Anand is ready to play the piano; if not, it's the trusty backing track. Some primary leaders have been known to play the guitar or even get a teachers' band together. It is fun for the staff and pupils to hear live music. So even if you're not yet able to play like your favourite guitar hero – have a go. You are modelling taking a risk, performing in front of others, collaborating and persevering. After all, that's what we ask our children to do, don't we?

What are the best songs for a primary school singing assembly? The official list – no arguments please!

1. 'This Little Light of Mine'
2. 'Autumn Days'
3. 'Cauliflowers Fluffy'
4. 'Saltwater'
5. 'From the Tiny Ant'

REFLECTIONS

- What for you are the key ingredients of memorable assemblies?
- How do you encourage all staff to be prepared to lead assemblies?
- How do you involve parents and governors in assemblies?
- To what extent can pupils plan, deliver and evaluate class assemblies?
- How can you entice keynote speakers to spice up the daily or weekly gathering?

BEHAVIOUR

Culture eats strategy for breakfast.

Peter Drucker

Your school culture as exemplified by the behaviour of children, teachers and parents sets the tone for how your school will run. Peter Drucker's much quoted phrase is not just a nifty soundbite. A school leader who sets a new direction of travel for their school without addressing necessary changes to the school ethos and culture is likely to stall and fail.

Simon Sinek (2014), a renowned thinker on leadership and management, inspired the idea that culture is:

Culture = Values + Behaviour

It is worth reflecting with your community each year on what you truly value and what this could look like in practice. Spend time with children, parents, teachers, support staff and governors on which values should become *our* values. Which ones are non-negotiable for our context? Which ones weave a tapestry of how *we* do things (or how we would like to do things) around here?

How do we move from a 'display on values in the school reception' to values coming alive in the broader culture of the school? Some effective schools ensure that a 'character curriculum' exists across the school day (Jubilee Centre for Character & Virtues, n.d.).

VALUES EMBEDDED ACROSS THE SCHOOL DAY

The journey to the classroom. What messages does the school send to pupils as they enter the building and walk to their classrooms every day? How clean and tidy is the school? Who is responsible for shared areas and corridor displays?

What is our focus this week or half term? Do I know as a learner what is expected of me, and is this consistent right across the school?

Registration could include a slide of this week's character focus (e.g. resilience). Lesson planning contains moments of learning which show what resilience means, for example, in maths, English, science, PE, break time, lunchtime and extracurricular activities.

Pupil behaviour is managed positively (until it can't be), reinforcing the school values (e.g. cooperation and empathy): 'You have been a good friend because… You are living our value of kindness. Thank you.'

Assemblies are carefully planned and programmed across the year to teach, model, celebrate and connect your school values internally and externally to your local, national and international communities. Visitors and visits to your community emphasise a child's place in and responsibility for 'your' school and town; social cohesion is enhanced, and service to others is embedded.

SUPPORTING BUSY TEACHERS WITH BEHAVIOUR PROBLEMS

When the senior leadership team (SLT) is observed following the school values of empathy, kindness and cooperation, then teachers will be more willing to raise expectations across the board. Few issues in school cause more division than behavioural issues seemingly dodged by senior staff to avoid confrontation with angry parents.

Ideally a school should have the following in place to support teachers with managing poor behaviour.

1. A vision, mission and set of values agreed by all.
2. A bespoke behaviour policy for your school and its contexts (what works down the road may not work here).

3. A home-school agreement between parents and the school on entry and re-signed annually. You may have to lean on these to show parents what they agreed to when choosing your school.
4. Training for all staff on how as a school we can live our values, model them and celebrate them.
5. A child-friendly behaviour flow chart that is in every learning space and shows what happens if expectations are not met. Of course, consistent implementation is the key to success. Highlight the positive too.
6. A team around the child approach to tackling repeated behaviours from individual pupils.

TEAM AROUND THE CHILD

For your most extreme cases involve a team of professionals to support the child to get back on track.

- Inclusion leader – can produce individual behavioural plans.
- Class teacher – can describe the before, during and after of episodes of difficult behaviour to better understand what's happening.
- Parents – can give you their take on what's happening and why. They may also be prepared to share updates on behaviour at home and any personal circumstances that might be helpful for professionals to know.
- A member of the SLT who can advocate for additional support, such as teaching assistant hours, or in extreme cases reduce the pupil to part-time until behaviours improve. A child may feel they have won here, and parents who are working may find this challenging; however, experience shows that the inconvenience factor can lead to a focus on improved behaviour for some.
- School counsellor – if your school is lucky enough to have a trained counsellor to help young people unpack what is behind the unwanted behaviour, this can lead to more sustained improvements.
- Educational psychologist – may uncover cognitive issues that are leading to behavioural outbursts.

- Social worker – if the family is working with a social worker, then they may have additional reflections on the context of the family which could help the school manage behaviour. (Would the child benefit from a breakfast club or after-school support?)

If the school can meet parents with compassion and without judgement, and enter into an effective partnership from which shared goals, objectives and improvements can be made, then you are in the strongest position for improvement. However, if parents do not support the school values at home, then come Monday morning the teacher feels they have to start explaining the expectations once more.

If the school has capacity, they could offer parenting workshops on setting boundaries at home, family literacy or specialist input on supporting pupils with attention deficit disorder or autistic spectrum disorder, for example.

Success lies in a clear parent–school partnership with shared values and expectations – one supporting the other. Where there are inconsistencies in behavioural standards, children eventually learn that expectations are contextual and will live up or down to these when set by different teachers at school, parents at home or coaches at football training.

BEHAVIOURS FOR LEARNING

The point of well-behaved children who are sociable and curious about the world is that they can achieve their very best and be positive members of our society.

The behaviour for learning conceptual framework (based on Ellis & Tod, 2018) sets out three relationships for learning: relationship with *self*, relationship with *others* and relationship with the *curriculum*.

In other words, first, self-regulation – how I manage my inner feelings, frustrations and distractions, which are informed by my self-esteem. Second, behaviours associated with peers, friends, teachers and others. Finally, how I engage (or not) with the learning, the texts, the projects, the classwork and the home learning. To what extent am I given responsibility for my own learning by harnessing my own interests, which might improve motivation and participation?

When the school culture and values support pupil behaviour and attitudes – such that children begin to grow in self-regard, enjoy taking responsibility and show their motivation through excellent attendance and engagement – then it might be said that the school has moved from managing behaviour to focusing in on behaviour for learning.

Headteachers who have experienced negative behaviours in challenging schools have reported the following:

1. That the SLT need to be visible and active in order that disruption is dealt with swiftly.
2. Repeat customers to 'refocus' time need support, mentorship and encouragement as well as clear consistent boundaries and sanctions.
3. Parents that are onside are your biggest allies; if they are not onside they can also be your biggest problem. Put in the time to build relationships with parents so you can work as a team for the benefit of their child. Send home positive messages as well.
4. Keep clear records and logs of behaviour incidents to support you in case you need to request additional support like teaching assistants.
5. Systems like CPOMS (Child Protection Online Management System) not only track safeguarding concerns but also behaviour and attitudes to learning, which can help give you an overview of hot spots or classes where you may wish to visit more regularly.
6. Pupil surveys like the Pupil Attitudes to Self and School (PASS) can provide a red, amber and green rated view of your children and what their needs might be in terms of their social and emotional wellbeing.
7. Positivity – catching children being good, greeting children every day and popping into lessons gives you authority that you can later lean on.

Remember, you might be the only consistent thing in some pupils' lives. You and your team have the power to improve life chances tremendously. Tell your team how special they are and, despite the challenges, to never forget what a difference they make.

ASIDE

STICKER CHARTS AND HOUSE POINTS VERSUS EDUCATION AS A REWARD IN AND OF ITSELF – DISCUSS.

Intrinsic and extrinsic reward systems in schools aim to impact on student motivation, engagement and academic performance. Who doesn't love a sticker chart, star of the week or certificates in assembly? However, it's worth asking ourselves: is this the right approach?

Intrinsic rewards, such as a sense of accomplishment, mastery and enjoyment derived from the learning process itself, some headteachers say, are considered vital for fostering long-term motivation and deep engagement in learning. Could it be that this approach correlates positively with academic success and lifelong learning habits and promoting a growth mindset?

On the other hand, extrinsic rewards, such as grades, praise or tangible incentives, are often used by teachers to motivate students in the short term. Experience indicates that these can be effective in prompting immediate behaviour change or compliance; their long-term impact on intrinsic motivation and learning outcomes is less clear. Some teachers suggest that excessive use of extrinsic rewards may undermine intrinsic motivation, leading to a decreased interest in learning for its own sake.

REFLECTIONS

- How do you reward children in your school?
- How much of this is in your behaviour policy?
- What is the balance like between intrinsic and extrinsic rewards?
- How do you reward your other stakeholders (teaching assistants, governors, caretakers, cleaners, local business owners)?
- Are you aligned with other local schools on practices like house systems?

CHILDREN

Education is not the filling of a pail, but the lighting of a fire.

William Butler Yeats

The one thing all teachers and parents can agree on is that children should be:

safe, happy, and learning.

How often do we as leaders in schools take the time to see school life through children's eyes? How clean is the school? How safe are the buildings and play equipment? Where do children feel safe, and where is scary for them? What of friendships and wellbeing?

One primary head spent several days shadowing pupils to see, for example, what it was like as a pupil with special educational needs and disabilities (SEND) through lessons, breaks, lunch and extracurricular clubs. What they realised was that all the efforts of inclusion in reality were turned into withdrawal sessions in empty rooms. That in fact for this child school was lonely, lacked variety and lost many opportunities for them to succeed.

As leaders we are asked daily if not hourly to make decisions: from the recruitment and retention of staff, to making the budget fit, to what training we should have, to preparing the community for inspection. One mentor of mine explained early on that all decisions in school could be viewed by asking:

What is best for the children?

Sounds simple. However, when you are faced with a deficit budget due to falling rolls and an expensive staff team, difficult decisions need to be made, especially when 'what is best for the children' is to retain and nurture your current happy, motivated staff – but you can't.

The role of leadership, if it is anything, is to build effective teams of people who trust each other to deliver towards a common goal. When you as the primary headteacher are faced with budgets that no longer work, and are set to worsen, then you and your governing body must reflect hard on your priorities, your team members, and what strategies you will adopt to keep the school viable and keep the community believing in the direction of travel of the organisation.

In primary schools, it is a truism that when headteachers are having 'one of those days' they will often decide to have a walk through the early years settings. Young children lost in a moment of curiosity, laughing, playing, thinking and collaborating reminds us of what our purpose is – namely, to lead learning. When children see an interested headteacher enter a space they usually come over to explain what they are doing and why – and would you like to try?

Not only is this a great decompression from the stresses of budgets, governance and inspections, to name but three, but it is a great opportunity to model the sorts of behaviours you want to see. From how you crouch down to talk to a small child, your tone of voice, the open-ended questions you ask and, importantly, how you praise effort over attainment: 'I can see how hard you've worked on this robot, Ray' – rather than 'Aren't you clever?' The message to all those eavesdropping – including the teacher – is clear: we value effort and resilience in our school.

THE EARLY YEARS

Primary leaders often refer to the 'magic of early years', and it is here that we shape youngsters positively with carefully considered learning environments and activities led by teachers, teaching assistants and the children themselves.

Early child development is a critical period in a child's life, which lays the foundation for their future physical, cognitive, emotional and social wellbeing. It is during these formative years that key elements such as secure attachments, emotional regulation, language acquisition and social skills are established. As educators, our role in championing children and guiding them to their best selves is paramount in ensuring they reach their full potential.

Attachment theory, pioneered by John Bowlby, is a captivating framework that highlights the profound impact of early relationships on child development. Imagine unlocking the secrets behind every hug, every comforting word and every high-five shared with your pupils.

It's all about nurturing secure bonds between children and caregivers, fostering a sense of safety and trust that serves as a foundation for their social, emotional and cognitive growth. By understanding attachment theory, primary school teachers can cultivate supportive classroom environments where every child feels valued, understood and empowered to explore the world with confidence.

If we add to this James Comer's dictum, 'No significant learning can occur without a significant relationship,' then as school leaders we must prioritise the way adults in the school relate and connect with pupils. How positive is your current behaviour policy in approach?

Emotional regulation is another key element of early childhood development. Children are learning to understand and manage their emotions, and as educators, we play a crucial role in teaching them how to express and cope with their feelings in a healthy way. By modelling positive emotional regulation strategies, providing a safe space for children to share their emotions and teaching them effective communication skills, we can empower them to navigate the complexities of their emotional world with confidence and self-awareness. The importance then of emotional literacy with children and staff cannot be overstated.

When children learn to control their emotions, rather than their emotions controlling them, they will learn how to be a good friend, team player and a reflective person, which will support more effective relationships as they grow into adult life.

Language acquisition, it seems obvious to say, is a critical aspect of early childhood development and sets the stage for future academic success and social interactions. As educators, we must provide rich language experiences through storytelling, conversations, songs and interactive activities that stimulate children's language development. By fostering a language-rich environment and encouraging children to express themselves creatively, we can support their cognitive growth and communication skills, laying a strong foundation for their academic journey.

Many of our schools will have populations of students for whom English is an additional language (EAL). School leaders should reflect on systems of support for these students from baseline assessments like the Common European Framework of Reference, which defines language acquisition from A1 (the lowest level) to C2 (completely fluent).

Most teachers will instinctively offer additional support materials, visual cues, key words and translated materials for pupils with EAL from their home language. Primary classrooms are particularly good at promoting speaking and listening, oracy skills through role-play, games, songs, questions and answers, and perhaps having a language buddy. Here, the children who speak other languages can teach some of their language to a partner. Where possible, having dual-language books, displays, labels and greetings will promote accelerated language acquisition while also supporting the child's mother tongue.

International schools which regularly have children from 50+ nations are particularly effective at driving forward with English while not forgetting to reference and pay respect to other countries, cultures and languages – much like the best inner-city schools in the UK.

Social skills development is also essential in early childhood, as children learn to interact with others, cooperate, resolve conflicts and empathise with their peers. As leaders, we can create opportunities for children to engage in collaborative activities, practice sharing and taking turns, and learn to respect and appreciate the diversity of perspectives and experiences around them. By promoting a culture of kindness, inclusivity and empathy, we can guide children towards becoming compassionate, socially competent individuals who can thrive in a diverse and interconnected world.

Primary-aged children are also PhD level at interviewing staff and identifying the 'kind one' or the 'funny one'. One head reports that they have a school council panel interview for prospective teachers, and they have yet to choose the wrong candidate.

When given authentic tasks and some guidance and responsibility children thrive.

ASIDE

HAPPY CHILDREN

For some children, schools are the only place that they will experience consistency, security and be exposed to music, art, drama and sport in a safe environment, not to mention breakfast clubs and school meals. With luck they will enjoy warm and respectful relationships with the school staff. The school then is a centre of intellectual enlightenment – outside of the algorithmic echo chambers of social media.

Have a laugh with the children! Children love mysteries, competitions, debates and (in appropriate fun contexts) throwing buckets of water/gunge on teachers' and especially headteachers' heads.

Some fun activities include:

- 'Alien fell to Earth' – get a teacher to dress up as an alien and arrange a UFO crash site in the playground. Organise a crash investigation, interview the alien, alien tea party, rebuild their spacecraft, newspaper report, podcast, visiting FBI agents...'We know it's you Mr Nourse.'
- Crime scene investigation – police tape, body shape taped on the floor, furniture upended, a whodunit?
- School disco/prom.
- Family picnics/BBQ/rounders game.
- House competitions.

- Art gallery – children organise programmes, make food, play music and read poetry – you can then auction off the pictures to parents for charity.
- Spelling bees.
- Nativity play.
- School productions.
- Bring-and-buy sales.
- Cake sales.
- Inviting in the grandparents – intergenerational projects.
- International day – learn about countries around the world.
- Sustainability events – sensory gardens.
- Book days, characters, authors and illustrators.
- Artificial intelligence (AI) day.

DELEGATION

...IT'S WHAT YOU NEED

> Leadership is the art of getting someone else to do something you want done because they want to do it.
>
> Dwight Eisenhower

When primary headteachers start to list the scope of their roles and responsibilities, it can be truly mind-blowing. The lengthy job description that accompanied the job advert seems daunting enough but, on the ground, and in the trenches, it is both humbling and energising.

You need to delegate.

The problem with becoming a headteacher for the first time is that most people have not really been trained to do it. If you are lucky, as a deputy head you had an experienced and generous headteacher mentor who gave you opportunities to manage budgets, governance, health and safety, performance management, teaching and learning, curriculum development, safeguarding, data analysis, self-evaluation forms, school development planning, community engagement, parental complaints, local authority/trust complaints, and HR issues with unions.

Most are not so lucky.

On top of this there is the human side of being the figurehead for a community. Much like a vicar you have to deal with, sadly, from time to time, bereavements, crisis and trauma. How much of this did you cover in your one-year PGCE? Training like the National Professional Qualification for Headship (NPQH) helps, of course; however, moving from theory to reality is quite a step up.

The Peter principle (Peter & Hull, 1994) is an observation that, in most organisational hierarchies, employees rise up in the organisation through promotion until they reach a level of relative incompetence.

One headteacher tells the tale of promoting her best teacher to year head and then later to deputy head, thinking that this amazing teacher would lead teaching and learning across the school and improve everything rapidly. Yet the truth was that this outstanding teacher in the classroom was viewed initially as overwhelming, unrealistic, a little arrogant and so did not take staff with him. In truth, he was not yet ready to lead – even though he was clearly the best teacher in the classroom.

New headteachers often try to do it all themselves. This is a mixture of enthusiastic zeal, not wanting to overload colleagues and wanting to control everything out of a fear of failure. The problem with this is that it leads to at least two problems. First, no one else has ownership of what is being controlled by the head – the classic example is 'I wrote the school development plan during the holiday – share it with the staff please.' If staff do read it, they won't necessarily understand why the priorities are there and what role they have in meeting the targets.

Second, and more importantly, this hero-head approach leads to exhaustion and burn-out. Most heads work long hours, have late meetings with governors and others, and often have a family of their own. To be able to sustain a successful headship careful delegation is required.

The answer lies in your strategy to build a high functioning team over years. How you decide to delegate the laundry list of activities that are needed to run a safe, happy and successful school is key. But it doesn't stop there. Once you are all clear on your roles, responsibilities and performance targets, that's just the starting line.

Here we come to the ABC of school leadership – a model influenced by a colleague who saw this on a police show on television – it is also the ABC of policing.

A is for assume nothing.

How many issues and mistakes in schools have been down to this one?

'I assumed the cover teacher would be on duty.'

'I assumed they knew what a learning objective was.'

'I assumed the parents would read the newsletter.'

It is worth reinforcing with your team that they should try not to assume anything in school and constantly anticipate a worst-case 'what if' position.

B is for believe nobody.

This sounds a bit harsh (in schools, maybe not in the police) and in reality, of course, trust with your team will build over time. Experienced headteachers will know that a 'show me don't tell me' approach gets to the heart of things quickly.

'Have you completed the scheme of work for Year 3 science – can you show me, please?'

C is for challenge everything.

'What can you expect from the kids around here?' – Challenge this low expectation.

'Special needs students by definition cannot make expected progress.' – Show the data that refutes this.

'Keep the parents at the gates!' – Model how effective parent partnership can improve pupil progress and the mood of those pesky WhatsApp groups.

'Ofsted single word judgements.' – Challenge the premise that all learning communities can be accurately summed up in the same way by a variable inspectorate.

- Challenge pupils to strive more – 'pedal faster' – attend more – engage more.
- Challenge parents to support teachers – 'help us help your child'.
- Challenge teachers to continue to grow professionally and be a better teacher this year than last. Support them with care, training and empathy.

Once you have delegated effectively you need to monitor and review progress.

In your weekly supervision sessions or review meetings, a culture of honesty is crucial. Model this for your team and praise it when you see it in meetings and emails. 'I don't know' and 'I need help with…' within a safe culture for leaders will ensure that the team honestly identifies gaps and works together to close them.

Teamwork makes the dream work!

The above motto turned into a lovingly mocked – 'Dad joke' – of a saying in one school. The staff enjoyed the cheesiness of it but also started to see that when everyone was aligned in where their energies were pointing, then impactful and positive change for children was indeed possible.

***

To be effective as a leader you must use every asset available to you. And choose wisely a style of leadership appropriate for a school's different stages of development.

LEAD FROM THE FRONT

Primary heads who have inherited a school in decline have reported that to start with they must adopt quite a dominant and dictatorial stance.

'This is not a democracy,' said one leader. 'Consultative, yes – but in the end the direction of travel is set by the leaders.' During this phase the following activities are often seen.

- Revisiting vision and mission.
- Refreshing the school values.
- Establishing a 'this is how we work together in this school' ethos.
- A motto is a great hook for your work and sets your strategic intention: 'Achieving together', for example.
- Raising expectations – challenging the status quo.
- Parents' meetings to tackle parents' concerns and start to foster a better home–school agreement.
- Set a few key priorities for all to work on – not a 100-page school development plan but a one pager. For example: 'Our key issues are reading, attitudes to learning and attendance. Activities: CPD on

phonics, shared and guided reading – buy books for book corners and a levelled reading scheme. Monitor progress against these few measurable activities weekly.'

LEAD FROM THE SIDE

- Work with your heads of phase and subject on key priorities that will impact pupils' attendance, happiness, safety and learning.
- Delegate more to your staff to form their own strategies and activities that support your learning objectives.
- Seek to grow capacity in middle leaders – push them to find answers and look into the latest educational research.
- Supervise your middle leaders regularly, and if you have an experienced deputy, they can also do this as they become familiar with your expectations

LEAD FROM THE BACK

It will probably take a number of years to move to this mode of delegation unless you inherit a high-performing team. Your role changes from leading the charge to that of being your own in-house His Majesty's Inspector (HMI). You provoke thoughtful discussions with leaders, governors, parents and pupils in order to smash any lingering glass ceilings.

You delegate aspects of most administrative and academic functions to capable and ambitious staff.

- Annual budget cycles can be shared – what other revenue streams could we build? Helpful governors with industry experience can also lead this.
- Recruitment – modelling interviewing for other senior staff to lead on. If there is something to get really right in a school, it is this!
- The servant leader – what do you need from me to make this happen?
- A culture of trust will mean that staff will drop in and ask for advice.
- Monitoring, evaluation and review led by the team and quality assured by you. Teams feeding back to governors on what they have

discovered about teaching and learning in their phases and what they propose the next steps should be.
- Set up groups of interested teachers to investigate new curriculum approaches (e.g. Curriculum with Unity Schools Partnership: https://www.unity-curriculum.co.uk; EAL approaches: https://www.coe.int/en/web/common-european-framework-reference-languages/level-descriptions).

The key to successful delegation is clarity around roles and responsibilities, key performance indicators and timelines. For instance: 'Can you please present to SLT in three weeks' time on an alternative approach to weekly planning formats in key stage 1. The aim is to reduce the time taken for teachers to plan, as well as further promoting progress in lessons. Feel free to check in with me at any time as you start to form your ideas.'

If you reflect on your current team, ask yourself who is hiding quietly in the corner of the staffroom who with the right encouragement and support could add real value to your school? Some heads remark on teaching assistants who lead on learning environments, amazing parents who lead on PTA events and fundraising, and pupils who lead on charitable events. Try delegating a development point to teachers who could join together in communities of practice to solve issues together to improve your school.

In the words of Craig Groeschel, 'If you delegate tasks, you create followers. If you delegate authority, over time, you will create leaders.'

ASIDE

Often in primary schools with small staff numbers you need to co-opt support from parents, governors and the wider community.

Helping Hands — volunteer group of parents to support hearing children read, making the props for a school play or even helping to build a school sensory garden over a weekend.

Governors can help with working with local authorities, trusts and teaching unions, on recruitment and retention, and celebrating the achievements of pupils and teachers.

Local businesses could also be persuaded to support your breakfast club, minibus fund, school trips, library improvements and updates to your IT equipment.

Parent groups also contain a huge range of experience and expertise; an audit of these can also provide you with a list of invested stakeholders who may well be ready to work on a project. One headteacher reports that a parent who worked with the Post Office was able, through their corporate social responsibility, to deliver much needed aid that the school had collected to a school in India.

- Where do you find your most reliable 'supporters'?
- Do you have in place 'delegation protocols', some guardrails for those supporting the school?

EMPATHY

> When the other person is hurting, confused, troubled, anxious, alienated, terrified; or when he or she is doubtful of self-worth, uncertain as to identity, then understanding is called for.
>
> Carl Rogers – American psychologist and champion of person-centred counselling

If you as a primary leader measure the amount of time each week you devote to the craft of teaching and learning, you may be surprised to find how little it actually is. Clearly, someone in your team needs to make classroom commerce their priority if you are otherwise preoccupied.

That's because you are the figurehead of a complex and ever-changing organisation – a ship on the educational sea buffeted by the tides of political opinion and deluged by the storms of events that happen weekly inside and near your school. Many of these events affect you and your staff and families deeply.

For example, take the headteacher whose communities face a collapsed building due to a storm and must reorganise into temporary buildings in 24 hours. In this critical incident, some staff said, 'It cannot be done,' angry parents asked, 'Why are we in this position?' and the children were confused as to what would happen next.

Empathy is the tool you reach for from your newly purchased *A–Z of Primary Leadership*. Why? Because to be able to relate and communicate with various stakeholders you must first understand where they are – and we do this through empathy and careful listening.

WHAT IS EMPATHY AND WHERE CAN I GET SOME?

During a debate on the merits of empathy in the classroom, one A-level history teacher claimed that 'empathy' was a shampoo for the over 40s!

> Empathy is the listener's effort to hear the other person deeply, accurately, and non-judgmentally. Empathy involves skilful reflective listening that clarifies and amplifies the person's own experience and meaning, without imposing the listener's own material. (Rogers, 1951)

The difference between the approach a counsellor might take and a headteacher is that at some point, once the issues have become clear, the headteacher might have to gently push back on a few assumptions, misunderstandings or untruths. However, if you have taken the trouble to sit authentically with a parent or staff member who is really upset, then that act in itself has already helped. How many times have we all thought when the red mist descends, 'You are not listening to me!'

Once you have reflected back to the parent or staff member their main concerns, so that you show you have listened and understood, you can then decide on what actions, if any, are needed. The best advice is that you end the meetings by saying, 'Will you come back to me in two weeks and let me know if what we agreed has been successful?' This is a powerful statement of the school's accountability and intent to improve collaboration with the parent or staff member.

The following is a similar approach to understanding and conflict resolution by Gerald Egan (2017). His work supports counsellors and human resources professionals. Egan's three-phase skilled helper approach as a framework for effective counselling and support within our educational community is well worth considering.

- Phase one, focusing on building rapport and exploring the issue, is crucial in understanding students' or adults' concerns deeply.
- Phase two, facilitating exploration and insight, encourages the development of critical thinking and problem-solving skills.
- Finally, phase three, planning and implementing change, empowers students and adults to take proactive steps towards resolution.

Harnessing Egan's approach equips educators to guide people through challenges effectively, fostering a supportive and empowering learning environment conducive to growth.

The skilled helper model, which emphasises active listening, empathy and structured problem-solving, can significantly inform performance management and personal growth. In performance management, it fosters a supportive environment where employees feel heard and valued, enhancing communication and resolving conflicts effectively.

By applying Egan's three-stage model – exploring the current situation, developing deeper understanding and formulating action plans – line managers can better assist teachers in addressing work-related issues and career development. For personal growth, Egan's approach encourages self-reflection, clarity in goal-setting and proactive steps towards personal and professional aspirations, ultimately leading to more fulfilled and engaged teachers within your school.

UNDERSTANDING BEREAVEMENT

Sadly, we will all be touched by bereavement, and in school you, as the headteacher, will find yourself talking to people from your learning community who are suffering a loss.

It can be very difficult to sit with people who are emotional and heartbroken by a recent death in the family – but if someone has decided to share this grief with you, it is a real honour.

- Listen attentively – being heard helps.
- Give time – no clock-watching here.
- Have tissues.
- Reassure them.

One headteacher who studied bereavement counselling shared the insights of William Worden (2009). His four tasks of mourning provide a useful way of understanding where people are on their journey.

It's worth noting that grief is a deeply personal and emotional experience, which is not linear – people (including children) can move forwards and backwards through any theoretical model. Time doesn't necessarily make things better – but empathy, understanding and connections can help.

1. Accept the reality of the loss – Often, soon after a death, relatives and friends can feel they are in a dream-like state – 'I cannot believe this is happening – I keep thinking I am going to wake up any minute.' Funerals play a key role in our culture to show everyone that this has happened, and we are marking this precious life together.
2. Process the pain of grief – Allowing oneself to feel and express the emotional pain of the loss. Some people avoid connecting with this pain and can use various methods to numb their feelings. However, unresolved grief placed in the emotional deep-freeze will wait for a time to express itself – sometimes years later – if not addressed. Counselling can really help start to process this pain.
3. Adjust to a world without the person – Adapting to life and finding new ways to live.
4. Memorialising the person – Ultimately, moving forward in life while honouring their loss.

Sometimes, schools have to face the death of a staff member or even a pupil. It is recommended that you seek *expert guidance* on how to manage this extremely sensitive time.

Professional counselling for staff and pupils can be very supportive in helping a learning community come to terms with what has happened. Some headteachers have chosen to memorialise staff by founding a scholarship, or naming a library, or simply having a fountain in the school garden. Other communities have built gardens of remembrance as a way of marking what has happened and providing a space in and around the school to think and reflect.

Managing bereavement in a school requires sensitivity, planning and clear communication to support students and staff. Your local authority or trust may well have crisis plans already in place. Here are some suggested guidelines.

1. **Consult** with your chair of governors and, when approved to do so, notify the community.

- Inform staff and students promptly with accurate and sensitive communication. Consider how to involve the bereaved family's wishes in the process.
- Provide immediate support through counselling services and designate a private space for those who need it.

2. **Communication**
   - Informing students – Age-appropriate communication is crucial. Younger children need simpler explanations.
   - Consistency – Ensure all staff deliver a consistent message to prevent rumours and misinformation.

3. **Support systems**
   - Counselling services – Offer on-site counselling and create a list of external support resources.
   - Staff training – Train staff on how to recognise and handle signs of grief and trauma in students.

4. **Memorial activities**
   - Commemorations – Plan respectful and inclusive memorial activities, such as a moment of silence, a memorial service or a dedicated space for tributes.
   - Involvement – Include students and staff in planning these activities to help them feel involved and supported.

5. **Academic considerations**
   - Flexibility – Provide flexibility with assignments and exams for grieving students. Offer alternative ways to complete work if necessary.
   - Monitoring – Regularly check in with bereaved students to monitor their academic progress and emotional wellbeing.

6. **Long-term support**
   - Follow-up – Ensure ongoing support for the bereaved over time, as grief can resurface.

- Anniversaries and significant dates – Be mindful of dates that might be particularly difficult and provide extra support during these times.

7. **Community engagement**
    - Parent communication – Keep parents informed about the school's response and available resources.
    - Partnerships – Collaborate with local mental health services and organisations specialising in grief support.

8. **Review and reflect**
    - Policy review – After a bereavement, review the school's policies and responses to identify areas for improvement.
    - Feedback – Gather feedback from students, staff and parents to improve future bereavement support.

Implementing these guidelines should help a school to provide a compassionate, supportive and effective response to bereavement, promoting healing and resilience within the school community.

ASIDE
RESOURCES

https://www.cruse.org.uk

https://www.winstonswish.org

https://www.mind.org.uk/information-support/guides-to-support-and-services/bereavement/support-and-self-care

https://www.macmillan.org.uk/cancer-information-and-support/supporting-someone/coping-with-bereavement

HELPFUL BOOKS FOR YOUNGER PUPILS ABOUT BEREAVEMENT

https://www.scholastic.com/parents/books-and-reading/raise-a-reader-blog/7-touching-books-to-help-kids-understand-death-and-grief.html

The Invisible String by Patrice Karst is a comforting story about two siblings who learn that everyone has an invisible string connecting them to everyone they love – anywhere, anytime – through separation, anger and even death: 'Even though you can't see it with your eyes, you can feel it deep in your heart, and know that you are always connected to the ones you love.'

Wherever You Are, My Love Will Find You by Nancy Tillman is a beautiful, heartfelt exploration of the unconditional love that a parent has for a child, even when they cannot be together. While death is not explicitly mentioned, this book is a lovely resource for offering reassurance to children who have experienced the loss of a parent.

Charlotte's Web by E. B. White is the classic story of Wilbur the pig and his amazing spider friend Charlotte who fills their lives with joy but ultimately passes away: 'After all, what's a life anyway? We're born, we live a little while, we die. A spider's life can't help being something of a mess, with all this trapping and eating flies. By helping you, perhaps I was trying to lift up my life a trifle. Heaven knows anyone's life can stand a little of that.'

Muddles, Puddles and Sunshine by Dianna Crossley is an activity book that offers practical and sensitive support for bereaved younger children. It has a helpful series of activities and exercises accompanied by the friendly characters of Bee and Bear.

FREE SCHOOL MEALS

Poverty is the worst form of violence.

Mahatma Gandhi

Some older readers may remember the chant 'Margaret Thatcher, Milk Snatcher' as reforms to school meals funding in the 1970s started to bite in a recession-hit Britain. The now infamous politician and first female prime minister of the United Kingdom cancelled the free milk programme for over seven-year-olds. This programme dated back to 1940 when children and pregnant women were issued with milk to prevent malnutrition during the food shortages of World War II.

In the 1980s, many school meal providers were privatised, perhaps leading to more commercial pressures being applied to the amount that was actually spent on the food on children's plates.

The work of Jamie Oliver (*Jamie's School Dinners* – Oliver, 2005) tackling the prevalence of processed food containing lower than desired nutritional levels (who can forget the dreaded 'Turkey Twizzlers'?) highlighted the poor quality of school meals. For some children this was their only hot meal of the day – so getting it right really matters.

More recently, Marcus Rashford, the England footballer, became famous for his tireless advocacy for free school meals for children in need. Initially he wanted to make sure that children had access to free school meals during the holidays, particularly the summer holidays during the COVID-19 pandemic, when they were not in school and therefore could not access school-provided meals.

It is shocking to all of us who work in schools with children from all backgrounds that many families today do not have enough food in the fridge or kitchen cupboards to properly feed their children.

The Royal College of Paediatrics and Child Health routinely reports that 'in a typical UK classroom 30% of children live in poverty'. They go on to say that poverty is associated with the following adverse effects:

- Poor health – including chronic conditions and obesity.
- Mental health problems – low self-esteem.
- Experience of bullying.
- Academic under achievement.
- Employment difficulties.
- Social deprivation.

> Poverty could mean you would not be able to live a 'normal kid's life' and might feel empty and useless. (Young person quoted at Royal College of Paediatrics and Child Health, 2020)

On average, 30% of our primary school pupils are at risk due to the poverty into which they are born. The government pupil premium grant is intended to be used to improve educational outcomes for disadvantaged children. If your school serves an area where parents are employed in the armed services you will be familiar with the service pupil premium.

One primary headteacher reports that a number of families in their school have not applied or registered for free school meals (FSM) even though they are eligible. The sense of stigma and shame that some families feel about this is palpable. Try to meet with these parents to let them know that even if they don't want the free school meal, the additional pupil premium funding will really help the school.

Don't forget that once a child is registered for FSM you may be able to claim pupil premium funding for up to six years.

Department for Education (DfE) (2025) funding for the academic year 2024/2025 is:

- Primary child: £1,480
- Secondary: £1,050
- Looked after children: £2,570

If you have a primary school of 420 pupils and have 100 pupils who attract pupil premium grants, your budget will have an additional £148,000. The question for you and your governors is how best to use this funding to support these children and, by association, others in their class?

What are the barriers to learning in your school? Poor attendance, low expectations, attitudes to learning, inconsistent quality of teaching and learning or inadequate provision for pupils with SEND and/or EAL?

Your team could usefully reflect on this excellent advice from *The EEF Guide to the Pupil Premium* (Education Endowment Foundation, 2024).

There are three common misconceptions about pupil premium funding:

1. Only applicable children can benefit from this funding. *Incorrect.* If you use the funding to improve teaching and learning across the school, then all pupils can benefit. A rising tide lifts all boats.
2. Pupil premium funding is only for the least able pupils. *Wrong.* High-achieving pupils who attract funding should benefit from interventions to support, stretch and challenge.
3. Pupil premium funding must only be spent on intervention strategies. *Not so.* In fact, a tiered approach to spending the grant is recommended:

    Step 1 – Identify your pupils' needs.

    Step 2 – Use strong evidence to support your strategy (EEF is a good place to start).

    Step 3 – Develop your strategy.

    Step 4 – Implement your strategy.

    Step 5 – Monitor and evaluate your strategy.

- How can governors support your work here?
- How can you coordinate strategies across a local cluster of schools with similar issues (perhaps shared teachers, inclusion assistants or teacher training)?
- Is there a place for a multi-academy trust attendance officer (in old money, the educational welfare officer – the eponymous EWO)?

- How can schools benefit from early interventions from multidisciplinary teams (i.e. health visitors, paediatricians, educational psychologists, speech and language therapists, occupational therapists, parenting classes, family literacy programmes and intergenerational programmes involving grandparents who may be caregivers)?

How should I use the pupil premium grant?

Fundamentally we want to improve the *achievement* of our disadvantaged pupils by working together. What do we mean by 'achieving together'?

Experienced headteachers report that there are five key drivers to better outcomes for children (see Figure 1).

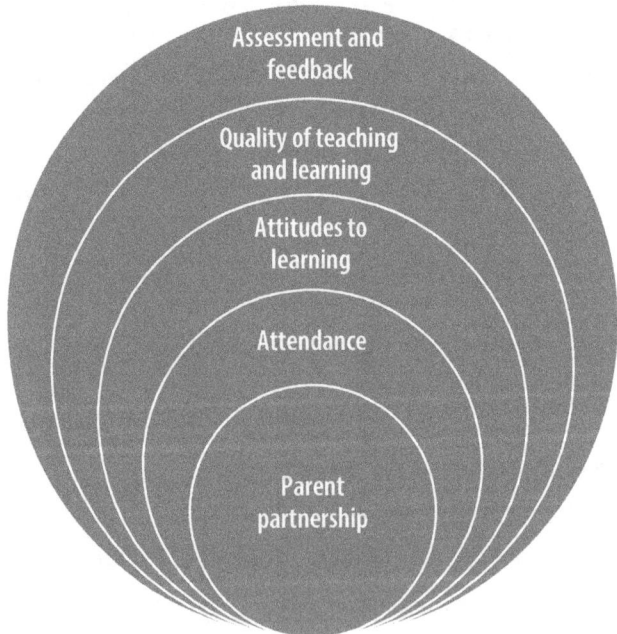

Figure 1. Five key drivers for school improvement

An activity for you and your senior team is: how could pupil premium funding support each of the following goals?

1. Parents understand the importance of their children attending school regularly and wish to be in a meaningful partnership with the school.
2. Children attend school at least 95% of the time. (Evidence suggests that students with the highest attendance achieve the highest grades at GCSE and A-level – see Department for Education, 2023.)
3. The school has clear expectations for behaviour based on values, and attitudes and behaviours for learning are taught and modelled. Pupil voice also supports the ongoing school improvement agenda.
4. Teachers are selected carefully and once inducted have a clear growth plan to constantly improve. Lesson observations, book looks and pupil progress data support both teacher appraisal and professional development needs.
5. Learners thrive in a positive environment with a rich mix of activities and learning experiences. Pupil wellbeing is constantly considered, and teachers, counsellors, teaching assistants and senior staff work collaboratively to safeguard and support young people. Personal goals are set termly, and older students research and evaluate their future plans – university and further education options are starting to be considered. (Yes, Year 6 is early, but why not start thinking about where all their hard work at school could lead them?)
6. Internal assessments are standards based and moderated to be at year-level expectations and beyond – leading to closer alignment to national and international benchmarks. Students with additional needs have adapted assessments to showcase their progress (learning pathways).
7. Teacher feedback both celebrates pupils' successes and signposts their next steps in learning.

BREAKFAST CLUB/AFTER-SCHOOL CARE

Headteachers report the benefits on attendance, behaviour and concentration of providing a before school breakfast club. When well managed this can also benefit staff who drop by for a quick piece of toast before the day starts – and pupils benefit from incidental conversations and understand the people behind the teachers' mask a little bit better.

Where connections can be made with local shops and supermarkets to sponsor the food, the long-term sustainability of such strategies can be assured. Staffing for this may come from the pupil premium grant – perhaps for a teaching assistant for an extra hour a day. SLT would be expected to routinely drop in by way of leadership by walkabout.

Setting this up like a home can make this time not only nutritionally effective but support the notion of *nurturing* some of the disadvantaged pupils.

> At its best, the nurture group was part of a genuinely 'nurturing' school, where all members were valued, but where this value was imbued with a rigorous drive for pupils to achieve their very best. (Ofsted, 2011, p. 6)

Read Ofsted's *Supporting Children with Challenging Behaviour Through a Nurture Group Approach* (2011) for some information on 'nurture groups'.

ADDITIONAL TEACHING ASSISTANTS

What does the research say about the impact of teaching assistants (TAs) on pupil progress?

Ask any teacher and they will unanimously say that TAs are a great support to both them and the children in the class. Now while it's true that if the trained teacher has more time to focus on children's learning thanks to an effective TA, then the children will benefit, there is also another side to that coin.

Although teachers, school managers and parents are largely positive about the contribution of TAs in classrooms, some research proposes that the current deployment and use of TAs in schools does not always lead to improved learning outcomes for all pupils (Webster & Blatchford, 2013; Webster & Blatchford 2015). However, there is good evidence to suggest that when deployed effectively TAs can have a positive impact on pupil learning (Bosanquet et al., 2016).

> The more interactions a pupil has with a TA, the less he or she is likely to interact with the teacher. (Avgerinou, 2019)

As a leader, you and your team will make decisions to deploy resources that you believe will have the greatest impact on your children's and in turn on their families' lives. You will read and digest research on the pupil premium. You will reflect. You will choose from options. You will keep under regular review the impact on pupils' wellbeing and their necessary progress to attain in line with all their peers.

The pupil premium has been a special gift to schools from government over many years now. As leading professionals, we must ensure this gift is not wasted and, indeed, is shown to be of real value.

ASIDE

CAN YOU AND YOUR TEAM DEFINE WHAT IT MEANS TO DEPLOY TEACHING ASSISTANTS EFFECTIVELY?

Teaching assistants support and nurture children every day. They are often the unsung heroes in a primary school as part of the dynamic duo in a classroom. Let's not as leaders assume that teaching assistants are well deployed, trained and appreciated but ensure they are.

How effectively are your teaching assistants deployed now? Who line manages them? How are they inducted and trained? What interventions are they responsible for? Do they always work with SEND students?

AND A PERSONAL ASIDE

I have first-hand experience as a parent of the power of well-trained teaching assistants. A year of regular reading intervention for my son who had struggled to read led to a breakthrough: old-school Toe by Toe.

He started to read. Thanks to Ms Angela's patience and insistence that he could do it, my son now reads beautifully. He uses technology to write but he can read, and that is probably the greatest gift that anyone will ever give him.

GOVERNANCE

> School governors are the unsung heroes of our education system. They are one of the biggest volunteer forces in the country, working in their spare time to promote school improvement and to support head teachers and teachers in their work. To date, governors have not received the recognition, support or attention that they deserve.
>
> Department for Education (2010)

The amazing thing about school governors is they have enormous responsibility, alongside the headteacher, for child safety, educational standards and the financial sustainability of the school.

Most are not from the education world but are stakeholders in the success of the school. This may be as parent governors, community governors or as governors related to a multi-academy trust, local education authority or faith organisation. They are volunteers who give freely of their time in meetings, committees, governor training and in schools supporting events and celebrating successes.

When you interview for your primary headship, you will meet the governors in several panel interviews, meet-the-staff sessions and when they finally offer you the job. Whether you decide to take the job will also be defined by how well you feel you can work with the governing body and, in particular, the chair of governors.

Are you on the same page educationally, and do you share a similar vision for the school and its community? Many colleagues have mentioned difficulties when working with their governing body. These have included micro-management, financial oversight that limited scope for significant change and, of course, personality clashes. It's worth making the point that you as a prospective head are interviewing the governing body just as much as they are interviewing you. It's a two-way selection process, and you must feel that ultimately you will have support as well as accountability from them.

The core functions of the governing body as defined by the DfE include:

- that the vision, ethos and strategic direction of the school are clearly defined;
- that the headteacher performs their responsibilities for the educational performance of the school; and
- the sound, proper and effective use of the school's financial resources.

GOOD GOVERNANCE = CRITICAL FRIEND

How do you start to build rapport with your governing body? Start with the chair and the clerk and map out your governance plan for the year ahead.

It's recommended to make sure that you have the right people on your governing body annually. An audit of skills will show you where any gaps lie. Each governor will have a professional background which could be highly impactful for a primary school.

While doing this, it is also important to ensure that all governors complete their pecuniary interest form to ensure there are no conflicts of interest when decision-making.

Governors also need to keep up to date with the latest DfE safeguarding policies. The clerk will keep a record of these for both good practice and inspection purposes. All new governors should have a clear induction programme that makes clear to them what their roles and responsibilities are, and what they are not (especially for parent/staff governors).

FROM DRAINS TO RADIATORS

I have been on the receiving end of parent complaints that were so well reasoned and presented that I thought, this is the kind of person I could do with on the governing body. In these cases, I have invited the complaining parent in for a cup of coffee and discussion of the issues. The issues could range from badly worded communications, dodgy car parks, concerns about SEND provision or how we might support gifted and talented children.

Experience shows that most people want to support schools to be even better, and when asked many people are keen to help. Not all will accept – but one parent with a business and customer service background supported us with timely parental communications in a more tactful way.

One parent who could be seen lighting up WhatsApp groups about car parking was skilfully brought onside to improve this; another with a strong background in SEND was approached to advise us and ultimately supported with the SEND committee of the full governing body. Bringing people back inside the tent is crucial.

If you are lucky – and shape your luck – parents who could drain the energy out of a meeting can begin to radiate positivity, partly because they now fully understand the issues the school is facing and partly because they want to be part of the solution.

INSPECTION

When preparing for any kind of external eyes or formal inspection with your governing body, apart from showing your minutes of meetings and headteacher performance management, build a case for the positive impact of your governing body – and the decisions they make.

> 369. Inspectors will seek evidence of the impact of the board of governors or the board of trustees. (Ofsted, 2024)

Evidence could include:

- Minutes of discussions on strategic planning – school self-evaluation.
- Documents outlining the school's vision, ethos and long-term goals.
- Records of governor training.
- School improvement and performance monitoring.
- Impact of pupil premium funding.

- Financial management – effective and efficient use of resources and additional revenue streams.
- Compliance and safeguarding.
- Support of SEND students.
- Stakeholder engagement.
- Governor visits and reports.
- Governors' impact on teaching and learning.
- Headteacher performance management.
- Recruitment and retention of quality staff.

A WONDERFUL CHAIR OF GOVERNORS

Let me tell you about Ina, who appointed a new deputy head. She had been a TV presenter and the general manager of a chain of successful businesses. Ina, who was in her 70s, was as sharp as a tack, totally community minded and the school's number one champion.

Ina read every report, every minute from committees and attended all chairs of governor training. Her approach to accountability when she employed this young deputy was: 'Thank you for all your flip charts on vision, and how you would lead the school's improvement. I will keep them and hold you accountable!' She did this with a twinkle in her eye and made sure that while the head and governors worked together to tackle underperformance, the school always felt that our 'critical friend' was a true friend.

When she nominated one of our teachers, Trevelyan May, for 'The Pearson Primary Teacher of the Year Awards', she was quoted in *The Guardian*: 'I've seen 'em come, and I've seen 'em go, but the one true greater-than-great teacher, the one most dedicated and committed to individual children, is Trevelyan.' Great praise indeed. And she adds that 'it is a true honour to serve our community alongside him' (Taylor, 2005).

This success was shared by the whole school community, and indeed schools where Trev went on to teach. But it was Ina, our chair of governors, who had the vision and experience to recognise and celebrate teachers who really commit everything to their pupils.

ASIDE
GLOBAL GOVERNANCE

As part of the prize of winning the primary teacher of the year, Trev was invited to go to Antarctica with Robert Swan. Trev, who hails from deepest Cornwall, was not so keen at first. He explained that he didn't like planes and usually the journey out of Cornwall to Hampshire was difficult enough. After some robust encouragement he agreed to go – and what a trip he had.

Robert Swan – the first man in history to walk to the North and South Poles – is a true inspiration. Many readers will remember the great French marine explorer Jacques Cousteau. Cousteau is credited with improving the Aqua-Lung design which gave birth to the scuba technology used today, and he was talking about environmental awareness and sustainability before it became mainstream.

Swan, in need of a patron for his expeditions, approached Cousteau who eventually agreed, but asked Robert to remove all sign of their presence from Antarctica after they finished. So it was that after a 900 mile walk that took 70 days Swan and his team arrived at the geographic South Pole, only to be told that their ship which was to take them home had just sunk. A short-lived triumph at the Pole then led Robert on something of an Odyssey (see https://www.robertswan.com).

Eventually, Swan did return with another ship and cleaned up tonnes of waste from Antarctica. Cousteau then asked Swan for a lifetime's commitment: 'Protect Antarctica, Robert – make sure that the world's last untouched wilderness remains unharmed.'

The treaty that protects Antarctica expires in 2041 and for the last 30 years Robert has been taking groups of young people from all around the world to see it, to be awestruck by its beauty and fragility. Then, on returning home, to preach the message in schools, in universities, in corporations and in governments 'Protect Antarctica'.

> Robert Swan is trying to invoke a kind of global governance for the good of the planet. A critical friend of business, governments and policy makers to see the long-term wisdom in conservation and global sustainability.
>
> - Do your governors adequately represent your learning community?
> - How do you train and deploy governors to support school improvement?
> - What happens if you have negative or disruptive governors? Who could support you?
> - Should you retain governors after their children leave your school?

HOLISTIC

Holistic: 'characterized by the belief that the parts of something are interconnected and can be explained only by reference to the whole'.

Oxford English Dictionary

Or to put it in the words of Aristotle: 'Educating the mind without educating the heart is no education at all.'

What are the various interconnected parts that make up the whole child?

The Michigan Department of Education (n.d.) has defined the whole child as '"a unique learner comprised of interacting dimensions such as cognitive, physical, behavioural, social and emotional". The whole child lives within multiple and interconnected environments including home, school, and community.'

What we see in schools is often children who can adapt, chameleon like, to different environments. If home is chaotic, some pupils will relish the order of clear expectations and routines at school, while others may not yet be ready to accept authority – and may play out the role models they have seen at home.

One head reports the story of Mary from an inner-city London school who was not concentrating on her English work during a Year 6 class. When asked why she was not concentrating, Mary said that the night before the police had chased the car she was in with her dad, and it had ended up on its roof. Dad had been arrested. Yet Mary had come to school and not mentioned anything until asked. Children have this ability to daydream and detach when real life gets too painful.

When we think about a holistic education, we consider cognitive, physical, behavioural, social and emotional aspects.

In the early years many think about the Montessori approach (see https://www.montessorimallorca.org/montessori-seven-principles). Maria Montessori was an Italian physician, educator and innovator, acclaimed for her educational method that builds on the way children learn naturally.

> The work of education is divided between the teacher and the environment.
>
> Montessori (1988)

One area that mattered to Maria was giving children agency.

Learning and wellbeing are improved, she argued, when children have a *sense of control over their lives* – children decide what to work on, how long to work on it, with whom to work on it and how to report back. This idea not only works but is scalable to any age group. The interplay between the learning environment and the knowledge and skills being learned were and are critical to an enriching experience. Other holistic experiences can also shape learning inside the brain.

THE NEUROSCIENCE OF LEARNING TO PLAY MUSIC

> The act of playing the piano is often seen as a captivating artistic endeavour that involves skill, emotion, and creativity. Beyond its aesthetic appeal, however, the practice of playing the piano also has a profound connection to the intricate workings of the human brain. This fascinating intersection of piano and neuroscience offers insights into how music engages the brain, promotes cognitive development, and influences our emotional well-being. (Xinyue, 2023)

Learning music in class as well as a musical instrument at home has been shown to have great benefits. Memory, concentration, spotting patterns, logic and reasoning as well as teamwork and collaboration when you play in a band or orchestra. The discipline of practising and learning a piece of music, but also understanding how to play with emotion and feeling, in time and in synch with other musicians, means that the brain lights up more with music than virtually any other activity.

FOREST SCHOOLS

Forest schools embrace the philosophy that the great outdoors is nature's best classroom, where kids can learn and play simultaneously. Picture children clambering over logs, building dens from sticks and getting gloriously muddy – all in the name of education! This approach fosters a love for nature, encourages creativity and builds resilience as kids solve problems like, 'How do I get down from this tree?' or 'Is this mud pie ready yet?'

Benefits include improved physical fitness from all that running around, enhanced social skills through teamwork (who else is going to help lift that heavy branch?) and a boost in confidence as they conquer new challenges. Further, there's the pure joy of discovering that, yes, frogs are indeed very cool, and, no, leaves don't taste very good. In essence, forest schools turn the wild world into a vibrant, hands-on learning experience that nurtures both mind and body, all while ensuring a fun-filled day in the fresh air.

DUKE OF EDINBURGH'S AWARD (AGE 13+)

The Duke of Edinburgh's Award (DofE) is all about turning life's adventures into golden (and silver and bronze) opportunities! Imagine a programme that says, 'Hey, want to become a superhero?' but instead of capes, you get maps, hiking boots and a volunteer badge.

The philosophy of DofE is simple: challenge yourself, discover new skills and have a blast doing it. Whether you're picking up litter, mastering the ukulele or scaling hills with a backpack half your size, every experience adds a new feather to your cap.

The benefits? First, there's the joy of achievement as you complete each level, which feels like levelling up in the game of life. You'll get fitter by doing physical activities, be it soccer or salsa. You'll become a community hero through volunteering, making the world a bit brighter one good deed at a time. Your brain gets a workout as you pick up new skills – ever wanted to juggle or bake the perfect brownie? Now's your chance.

And let's not forget the expeditions! Think of them as epic quests where you and your fellow adventurers navigate the wilderness, find treasure (or at least the next campsite) and share stories by the campfire. At gold level, there's even a residential section where you can bond with new friends over shared activities.

In short, DofE is like life's greatest hits rolled into one programme. It's fun, it's rewarding and by the end, you might just feel like you've conquered the world – or at least a really big hill.

CHARITY AND SERVICE TO OTHERS

Service-led activities in UK primary schools can be a fantastic way for children to have fun while making a positive impact on their community. Here are a few ideas:

1. Litter heroes: Armed with grabbers and gloves, children become litter heroes on a mission to tidy up the playground or local park. With capes fluttering in the wind, they swoop in to capture every stray crisp packet and sweet wrapper, turning their neighbourhood into a cleaner, greener place.

2. Garden gurus: Children can roll up their sleeves and become garden gurus, transforming a patch of the school grounds into a blooming paradise. Planting flowers, vegetables and even a tree or two, they learn about nature while getting their hands delightfully dirty. Plus, they might spot some friendly worms!

3. Reading buddies: Older students pair up with younger classmates as reading buddies, sharing their favourite stories and embarking on imaginative adventures together. With each turn of the page, they help to foster a love for reading and build strong friendships.

4. Crafty crafters: Children can unleash their creativity as crafty crafters, making cheerful cards and decorations for local care homes or hospitals. Armed with glitter, glue and a rainbow of coloured paper, they spread joy and brighten someone's day with their handmade masterpieces.

5. Fundraising fun: Organise a charity challenge where pupils come up with wacky ways to raise money for a good cause. Whether it's a silly hat day, a sponsored hop-a-thon or a talent show, children can let their imaginations run wild while learning the importance of helping others.
6. Pet protectors: Teaming up with a local animal shelter, pupils become pet protectors. They can collect donations of food and toys, make cosy blankets and even write stories or draw pictures of the animals to help them find forever homes.
7. Eco warriors: Young eco warriors can embark on projects like building bug hotels, creating recycling stations or starting a compost bin. They learn about sustainability and how small actions can make a big difference for the planet.

These activities not only teach valuable lessons about responsibility, teamwork and community spirit, but also ensure that children have a blast while making a positive impact on the world around them.

SOCIAL AND EMOTIONAL WELLBEING

Promoting social and emotional development in primary-aged children is crucial for their overall wellbeing and future success. It helps them build strong relationships, manage emotions and develop empathy. Strategies include encouraging cooperative play, teaching emotional vocabulary and modelling positive behaviours.

Create a supportive classroom environment where children feel safe to express themselves. Incorporate activities like role-playing and group discussions to enhance social skills. Praise positive interactions and provide gentle guidance during conflicts. By fostering these skills early, we empower children to navigate life's challenges with confidence and compassion.

ASIDE

What makes holistic education so impactful? Try this example from a junior school in Southampton.

Each year, the Year 6 classes and teachers travel to an outward-bound centre in France. Among the team-building adventures there were also field trips. The most memorable was to visit the D-Day beaches.

A team of thoughtful teachers had already taught the children about Britain since the 1930s and pre-taught all about 6 June 1944. A reflective hush fell over the pupils as they walked into the military cemetery a few hundred metres from Omaha Beach. The staff gave each child a flower and asked them to place them on a grave that for some reason caught their attention.

The children found many interesting names and backgrounds on the gravestones – but those who brought a tear to the eye were the ones who had found a young soldier who shared their family name and had decided to place their flower beside that stone.

Amazing history learning with a real context – and the children exhibited high levels of empathy and emotional literacy.

1. How can we teach children about emotional intelligence?
2. To what extent can we enhance pupil's oracy skills through opportunities to speak about art, music, dance and poetry linked to areas of learning (e.g. current affairs or people and events from history)?

INSPECTION

Say 'Ofsted' to teachers and the first thing you normally read in their expression is fear. Why is that?

Are they afraid of being found out as a bad teacher, even though they are fine teachers? Are they worried about the additional workload that might be dumped on them if they know the school will be inspected this year? Are they anxious that they will let the team down, let the school down, and let the children and parents down?

It could be all of the above and more. I have seen ECTs relish inspection and invite inspectors to see 'an amazing science lesson', but likewise I have seen experienced and capable colleagues buckle under the weight of these high-stakes audits.

As a headteacher you will be hoping for a competent and experienced team who will work alongside you and your community to deliver a fair and developmental report which will support further improvements.

FIVE P'S – PLANNING AND PREPARATION PREVENT POOR PERFORMANCE

Ensure you have the following ready:

1. Self-evaluation form (SEF) – strengths and weaknesses – involve your whole community in this – you may find out things you didn't know.
2. Pupil progress data – three years' worth at least – internal and external with assessment policy. Show progress and attainment of different groups of learners. Show how pupil numbers are

changing over time and how the cohort is made up (EAL, SEND, boys and girls, more able pupils).
3. School improvement plan (SIP) – linked to what your SEF and data packs are telling you. Set ambitious goals for the school. Subject action plans can sit under this document.
4. Safeguarding/child protection policies – single central register – safer recruitment.
5. Curriculum planning – scope and sequence of what is taught in the subjects across the school.
6. What is the progress of the bottom 20% of readers? What is working, and what is not?
7. Teacher performance management – to what extent teachers meet goals around (i) pupil progress (e.g. 90% of students are meeting expectations in English), (ii) reading target, (iii) quality of teaching and learning, and (iv) professional development target (e.g. completed National Professional Qualification for Senior Leadership).
8. Governance structures, subcommittees aligned with SIP priorities. SEND governor, safeguarding lead – strategic direction – yearly governance plan. Minutes of meetings.
9. Attendance records and evidence of actions and impacts on families with low attendance.
10. Parent and pupil feedback (e.g. surveys, pupil voice, parents' groups, PTA, parent volunteers, newsletters, assemblies, year books, parent information meetings and handbooks).
11. SEND reports that present case studies of how you meet additional needs.
12. Pupil premium funding and how you spend this effectively to improve attainment and progress.
13. Behaviour records – including any exclusions.
14. Your in-house monitoring, evaluation and review.

This should include the holy trinity of lesson observations, book looks and progress data. A good inspector will say, 'Show me the best practice you have in your school'. They are testing to see if you know your school, if you know what very 'good' or 'outstanding' teaching looks like and how consistent this is across age groups.

OVERWHELMING STAFF

What can happen when the pressure is on, for headteachers and senior leaders, is they can panic and start to throw the kitchen sink at teachers, teaching assistants and support staff. While this is understandable, and all schools want to do their best, overwhelming the team during a stressful week will ultimately be counterproductive.

So, what's the answer?

Try to be (particularly) inspection ready when you know your school is likely to be inspected in terms of timeframes set out by the national inspectorate.

Ten top tips to support you when an inspector calls

1. What happens when you get the phone call – have your script and checklist to hand for the extended conversation with the lead inspector.
2. Summary SEF and SIP with a few school-wide priorities.
3. Learning environments – really 'singing their subjects'.
4. Books – well presented, showcasing progress over time – feedback evident.
5. Planning – if learning is really evident in lessons inspectors may not dig far into planning; if not, they are likely to want to understand in more detail how the learning journey is structured to meet all needs.
6. Timetables – make sure they are up to date and mention any issues like long-term supply cover.
7. Governors – inform them immediately and meet the chair as soon as possible to share the outline of the visit and when governors are expected to attend.
8. Parents – inform parents in a positive way that the school will have some visitors and that their views will be sought.

9. School council – brief them on the visit and explain that their views are important to help the team further support the school. The final selection of the group to meet the inspector is left to your discretion!
10. Pupils – in assembly, explain what will happen during the visit and why it is happening. Emphasise the importance of being on time and doing their best in lessons and at break times, 'just as you always do!'

LEADING THE INSPECTION

The whole learning community will be looking at how you are processing this inspection to inform them how they will process the inspection. So, be positive, be confident, use a little humour and note that 'We are all going into this as a team – let's work hard for each other and show them how great our school is. There will be areas that will need further improvement after the inspection – there always are. However, we are proud of how far the school has come, and we are proud of our pupils, families and our staff as we are "achieving together".'

Most inspectors are ex-colleagues who know what it's like to be under the microscope. The best will work alongside you, encourage joint observations, discuss your context and challenges, and work hard to evidence the best grade they can for your school.

Therefore, it is crucial that you cultivate a positive working relationship with the lead from the get-go.

As part of your usual monitoring schedule, you and your team will doubtless consider the following areas on a regular basis, so an inspection will present no – or very few – surprises.

- Impact of teaching on learning.
- Do you see what I see (joint learning walks and lesson observations)?
- What do the books tell you (attitudes to learning, quantity, quality, scaffolded learning, and stretch and challenge for all)?
- What do the pupils tell you? (Can they recall what they were taught last term? Attitudes to learning, what helps them learn best, what do they think the school should improve on?)

- School reception – values, vision and mission (first impressions count).
- Journey to the classroom – corridors, displays, music, smells, behaviour.
- Consistency in classrooms – display, pedagogy, technology.
- Language of learning (e.g. key questions, objectives, 'I do, we do, you do' model, plenary – peer support, peer feedback).
- Attitudes to learning – lesson starters, pace, engagement, activities, questions and answers, pupil-led learning, behaviour for learning.
- Ethos of school – school values visible in displays, lessons, assemblies and in the behaviour of learners and teachers.

SUPPORT FOR HEADTEACHERS

Inevitably, the focus of any school inspection will turn to the effectiveness of the headteacher and governors. When the inspection report tells the world the school has improved or remained 'outstanding', then the community celebrates. However, when the report downgrades a school or puts it down as 'inadequate', the impact is profound.

I think it's important to mention the tragic death of Ruth Perry who was a primary headteacher: 'The coroner's report found that the inspection contributed to the cause of her death. The case added significant weight to calls for full system reform of inspection' (NAHT, 2024a).

We were all shocked by Ruth's death after her school was judged by Ofsted to have declined from 'outstanding' to 'inadequate'. The immense pressure and stress she must have felt is unimaginable. Her case shines a light not only on the current inspection process, but also on the relentless day-to-day pressure that teachers and headteachers face in our schools.

As a profession we have a duty to ensure that headteachers' and teachers' mental health is properly supported, especially before, during and after an inspection. But more than that, doesn't it tell us that this approach to the 'quality assurance' of education needs significant improvement? Imagine summing up someone's life's work in a single pejorative.

The NAHT published *Rethinking school inspection: Delivering, fair, proportionate and humane school accountability* in January 2024, and the fact that they use the phrase 'humane school accountability' really does show how negatively impactful Ofsted inspections can be. Please do take some time to read this and discuss with your governing body.

CODA

The Office for Standards in Education, Children's Services and Skills (Ofsted) was created following the Education (Schools) Act 1992. The various inspection frameworks which have followed over three decades have reflected the priorities of chief inspectors and of the government of the day.

The framework of recent years has put a particular focus on the curriculum which leaders and teachers have welcomed. Now a new 'toolkit for self-evaluation and inspection' is emerging; trial inspections are happening as this book goes to press.

School inspection frameworks, wherever they operate in the world, make judgements about the following key aspects:

- Pupils' achievement, attendance, behaviour and personal development.
- Inclusion and safeguarding.
- Teaching and learning.
- Curriculum.
- Leadership, management and governance.

Inspectors and reports record whether the above aspects meet, exceed or fall below nationally expected standards. For the interest of parents and the system generally, the best frameworks also applaud excellence and exemplary practice; and, where needed, identify the handful of schools and settings where urgent intervention is required in the best interests of the children.

Whatever framework is in operation, leaders and teachers make it work for their children, their families, their communities. There is always so much good and great practice to be proud of in our schools. And all the advice set out in this chapter will be relevant as long as formal inspection by an external party exists.

The author's own view is that rigorous self-evaluation lies at the heart of primary leadership and is the starting point for school improvement.

> # ASIDE
>
> If the goal of school inspections is to ensure that all children are safe, happy and learning appropriately, then other approaches to inspection are worth considering.
>
> ## SUPPORTED SELF-EVALUATION
>
> Southampton Unitary Authority used the supported self-evaluation approach in the 2000s. A local education officer, who in one case was an HMI, would visit the school termly and together they would evaluate parts of the school. It was challenging, involved all stakeholders and ultimately helped to clarify the 'ground truth' of the school. This helped to shape the school's priorities and training needs. It held the SLT and governors accountable, but it didn't shame them – it supported them.
>
> > 'Inspection should not be about judgement, failure and condemnation, but more about a constructive, professional and helpful dialogue.' (NAHT, 2024b, p. 10).
>
> - What are your and your leadership team's current thoughts and ideas about how Ofsted should approach inspection and self-evaluation in the years to come?
>
> ## AN INSPECTOR CALLS CURRENT CHECKLIST
>
> During the initial phone call from Ofsted inspectors to a school, several key pieces of information are typically discussed to help prepare for the upcoming inspection. Here are some common topics and questions that inspectors might cover:
>
> 1. Confirmation of inspection dates: Inspectors will confirm the dates of the inspection and outline the schedule.
> 2. Purpose and scope of inspection: An explanation of the focus and framework of the inspection, including specific areas of interest.

3. School context: Inspectors may ask for an overview of the school, including:
- Number of pupils and staff.
- The school's demographic and any significant changes or challenges.
- Current priorities or recent improvements.
4. Recent developments: Any major changes since the last inspection, such as new initiatives, leadership changes or significant events.
5. Key documents: Inspectors will request key documents to review, which might include:
- The school self-evaluation form.
- The school improvement plan.
- Recent performance data.
6. Safeguarding: Initial questions about the school's safeguarding policies and procedures.
7. Logistics: Arrangements for the inspection, such as:
- Meeting times with senior leaders, governors and other key staff.
- Classroom observations and timetable.
- Availability of rooms and facilities for inspectors.
8. Concerns and queries: Any immediate concerns or questions from the school's leadership about the inspection process.

This initial call is intended to ensure that both the school and the inspectors are well-prepared, and that the inspection can proceed smoothly and effectively.

JOURNEY

A great captain leads with a steady hand and an open heart.

Anon.

As you start the academic year, safe in the harbour, preparing for the long and arduous journey ahead, the above quote can be helpful. It encapsulates the essence of balanced leadership, combining firmness and empathy to guide your crew and passengers effectively through the challenges ahead.

PLANNING YOUR JOURNEY: THE FIVE P'S

Planning and preparation prevent poor performance.

What sort of plans and maps should we have to help us navigate safely on our journey?

Your twelve core documents will include the following:

1. Yearly calendar with major events and performance management arrangements identified, including monitoring evaluation and review, data drops, parents' meetings, reports, productions, sports days and teacher training.
2. Schedule of meetings – SLT, mid-level leadership team, staff meetings and how these feed into each other.
3. Termly CPD planned to meet performance management and school improvement plan needs.
4. Governors' yearly work planner – meetings, visits, celebrations and how subcommittees support the school improvement agenda.

5. Latest school improvement plan – and a summary to share regularly.
6. Data pack to show the progress towards targets and where further improvement might be needed as a school, by subject, year group, subgroups and Level 3 year trends.
7. School plan – roomings – who goes where.
8. Timetables – check you are compliant with guided teaching hours per subject.
9. Class lists – try to balance needs.
10. Rotas and routines for your setting, including assembly themes that support your values, bus arrangements, early and late children supervision.
11. Staff handbook – a quick start guide to teaching at your school.
12. Child protection policies and designated specialist provision.

Start the voyage with the end destination in mind. If you need to raise attainment, then set some challenging targets with your teams and communicate them at every opportunity to parents, to pupils and to staff. Start your weekly staff briefing with some telling examples of strong practice in your school and how this is contributing to pupils meeting their targets. Thank staff for the extra work they do on displays, shared areas, extracurricular clubs and sporting activities.

Remind support staff how valuable they are in ensuring that the ship keeps sailing purposefully towards the final destination.

Teamwork makes the dream work.

Whatever your pupils' starting points, and many will be low, the truth is that they need to reach the expected outcomes for their year group. What of SEND learners and EAL learners, I hear your cry? Admittedly, a small group of learners will not reach the target, but shall we say this is 10% of your community?

Therefore, a challenging target for your crew will be to get 90% of pupils to expected levels or better. 'We could never do that in our school.' Some teachers might say this, and it is only right that we acknowledge the huge pressures on some schools – for instance, a high percentage of pupil premium students, a transient student body, disengaged parents, low expectations, poor attitudes to learning, high teacher turnover, falling rolls and budgets. No one said this would be easy. If it was easy, it would have been done by now.

However, some schools in the most difficult of circumstances manage to do this year after year. If you look at examples in rural, coastal and urban settings across the UK you will see astonishing pupil attainment from very low starting points. How do they do it? Top levels of attainment are rooted in unambiguous high expectations (not 'aspirations'), a 'no excuses' culture, consistent implementation of agreed practices, and a precision and purpose to everything.

Further, leaders harness the crew network effectively and learn from each other.

Michael Fullan's concept of 'networked learning communities' (NLCs) has garnered significant attention for its transformative impact on schools and teachers. The most successful academy trusts – small and large – embody this way of working.

NLCs encourage collaboration, continuous improvement and the solving of common problems. They are the FAQs of the teaching world! They provide a platform for schools to share best practices, innovate and support one another.

By connecting teachers across different schools and authorities/trusts, NLCs create a supportive environment where teachers can share experiences, strategies and resources. Some of the most powerful and welcomed continuing professional development comes from credible colleagues doing the same job as you.

These professional groups when organised and invested in – in terms of time and a modest budget – can identify areas for improvement and implement evidence-based strategies. This continuous cycle of reflection and action can create a culture of accountability and excellence. If led well, these networks ensure that teaching practices are adapted with the latest educational research in mind.

***

So, with the preparations complete and the crew feeling supported in their professional networks, you set sail and steer your ship towards your destination of higher attainment, better attendance and higher expectations for all.

But…You suddenly spring a leak in the ship, you lose a crew member and the passengers are getting seasick as the storm approaches. What should you do?

In the words of the World War II British government poster, 'Keep Calm and Carry On'.

Gather your leadership team, and possibly your chair of governors, to assess the impact of what has happened and what is likely to happen soon.

Think in short-, medium- and long-term solutions.

For example, the leaking ship can be packed with cork (short term), running repairs made at the next harbour (medium term), and section of deck removed and replaced in dry dock (long term).

Back-to-school scenario: Member of staff leaves suddenly. Deputy covers for two weeks (short term). Meanwhile, advertise for two-term cover which could go permanent (medium term). Appoint a full-time replacement (long term).

Communicating with staff and parents at every stage is vital to stop the WhatsApp groups overheating: 'This has happened, we have a plan and we will keep you informed.'

For big issues, you will want to hold a parents' coffee morning to take any additional questions. Being seen to be transparent and honest is the key here. If you are asked a question and you don't know the answer, it is all right to say so, but ask someone to take note of any pending queries so you can answer them as soon as possible, perhaps in the next newsletter.

One primary head described her monthly 'meet the headteacher' meetings as feeling 'boiled in oil'! However, as uncomfortable as some of these can be, they will get easier as parents relax with you, trust you and seek to support rather than criticise the work of the school. But please remember that you cannot please all the people all the time – and on your journey you must be guided by your compass, which always points to 'what is best for the children'.

So, the storm has passed, the wind is set fair in the sails and you can see land in the distance. As your journey starts to come to an end, it's a good idea to review and evaluate how well the crew and passengers have fared.

For your senior staff, how have they led their departments, met their goals and kept morale high? For middle leaders, what impact have they had on teaching and learning, on pupils' progress and, ultimately, their end-of-year attainment?

Schools are normally quite good at writing developments and putting on training but less good at evaluating the impact (see Education Endowment Foundation, n.d.).

WHAT GETS MEASURED GETS DONE!

In your evaluation of the school's year, go back to your vision, your school improvement plan, your budget, your pupil data, your performance management arrangements, your stakeholder surveys and your pupil interviews.

1. To what extent is your school delivering on your vision – how far along the way are you on reaching the ideal school environment that you all signed up to?
2. Put a day in your diary, go offsite if you can with your team, to honestly judge if you have met or partially met your targets. What were the pain points, what worked well and what didn't? What have you learned?
3. To what extent are your teaching staff more effective this year than last? How is morale? Do people feel valued, and do they feel they contribute to the success of your school? Has training worked, or were the doughnuts the highlight of most staff meetings? What do your team say about their wellbeing? What would help?
4. Listen to the voices of your stakeholders – even in a complaint there will often be a grain of truth that will help you shape your school. What are you proud of as a school, and how can you build on these areas further?

5. Talk to your children – from them can come an innocent wisdom that transcends the staffroom banter, challenges the status quo and can reveal how school impacts them. (King James Bible, Psalms 8:2, 'Out of the mouth of babes and sucklings hast thou ordained strength.')

ASIDE

The early years foundation stage are masters at this cycle: plan – do – review (keep it simple, stupid) (see Figure 2).

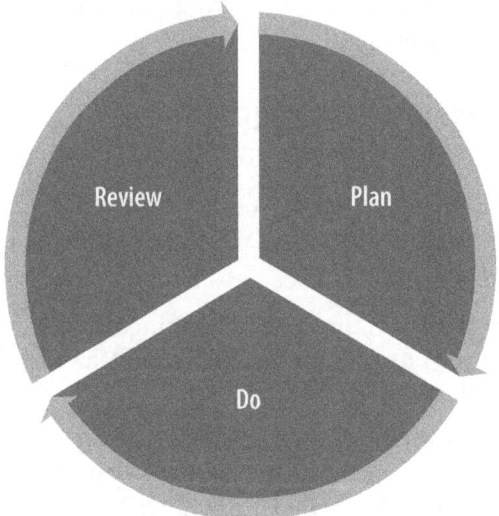

Figure 2. Early years practice

If you can't explain it simply, you don't understand it well enough.

Albert Einstein

REFLECTION

1. What have been your successes with leadership at all levels?
2. What are you particularly proud of?
3. How have you refined your practices over time?

KINDNESS

Primary teachers love the children, secondary teachers love their subject, and university lecturers love themselves!

Anon.

When you ask primary children why they like their teacher they will often say because they are kind. (Think Miss Honey from *Matilda*.) In leadership, too, kindness is important as it helps to build trust and rapport with your whole learning community. The phrase 'Don't mistake kindness for weakness' encapsulates a powerful message, emphasising that kindness, while gentle and compassionate, should not be underestimated or perceived as a lack of strength.

This sentiment is often reflected in the actions and leadership style of figures like Jacinda Ardern, the former prime minister of New Zealand.

LEADING WITH EMPATHY

Ardern's approach to her premiership was characterised in crucial moments by her natural empathy. The Christchurch mosque shootings in 2019 shocked the world, but it was her compassionate response – marked by immediate support for the victims and a call for unity and love – which resonated globally. She wore a hijab while visiting the grieving Muslim community, a gesture of respect and solidarity that spoke volumes. This act of kindness and her heartfelt words showed a leader who was not afraid to show vulnerability and humanity in the face of tragedy.

As leaders it is okay to show that we are not perfect, that we can make mistakes and that we are also moved by events locally, nationally and internationally. This sends a powerful message to our team that we are only human, but the team – a well-oiled machine, honest, reflective, driven and empathetic – will meet all challenges effectively.

RANDOM ACTS OF KINDNESS

A few years ago, I was having lunch in a restaurant with my wife, and I was not concentrating on what she was talking about – a dangerous pastime. Instead, I was trying to listen to the table of older men behind me as they discussed their experiences from World War II.

One was a pilot who had flown Hurricane fighters. He was explaining how he loved flying this aircraft, and when he was told he would be getting a new aeroplane he refused. His commanding officer explained that the new fighter was very good, and he should give it a try. It was the Spitfire. Another man had been a London air raid precautions warden during the Blitz in 1940. Another had been in the Burma campaign. The last, a man called Jack, had been evacuated from Dunkirk and fought in North Africa and Italy.

I whispered to my wife that they were all World War II veterans. Without a thought, she said we should pay for their lunch, without telling them, as a random act of kindness. I agreed. As we left and settled the bill, the waiter took my phone number in case it was needed. Later that day, the restaurant phoned me to say the gentlemen were so happy and would like to get in touch.

As a result, for several years after, they all came to the primary school where I was headteacher as speakers about Britain since the 1930s. They told their stories, enjoyed our VE day street party and, just for a few hours, they were pilots, policemen and soldiers again – but this time safe and sound, surrounded by curious children keen to listen and feed them with homemade Victoria sponge cake.

All it took was a little kindness.

Isn't it true that when you take time to listen to people and show some kindness and empathy that everyone has a story to tell? So often through a random meeting a connection can be made to benefit the school. Although headteachers are always busy, making time for people will pay back handsomely.

> # ASIDE
> ## SYDNEY CHARLES PIGDEN
> (London Borough of Lewisham – World War II Spitfire pilot, teacher, football coach)
>
> Please watch the following video link: https://www.youtube.com/watch?v=6caCqn_nD6o.
>
> This teacher's kindness had a huge effect on one young man from a tough background in South London. That young man could not control his temper, concentrate in class and had difficulty reading. But with the kindness of his teacher – who understood his 'heeby-jeebies', taught him to read, and made him responsible for giving out the registers and being a class monitor – something changed.
>
> The boy was Ian Wright who would grow up to be an Arsenal and England footballer of legend. Reflecting on the impact of Mr Pigden's kindness, Ian said that his teacher gave him self-worth and made him feel important. Years later, Ian still thinks about his old primary school teacher every day and understands that the encouragement he received changed his life.
>
> The lesson: never underestimate the power of kindness that you show your children and their families.

LEADERSHIP

> Never doubt that a small group of thoughtful, concerned citizens can change the world. Indeed, it is the only thing that ever has.
>
> Margaret Mead

THE GOOD

Let me tell you about one teacher's experience of a really good headteacher called Peter:

> He was my first headteacher when I was an NQT. Peter was a friendly and kind middle-aged man with a background as a primary adviser. He was an 'attention to detail' leader who set clear expectations for us. He was visible before and after school – and would drop into lessons from time to time.
>
> 'Always stand at the school gate – you get to know the parents, siblings who are coming through and can nip small issues in the bud quickly and easily,' advised Peter.
>
> When I had a parent complain that I wasn't challenging their more able child enough he supported me – directed my practice and managed the parents with confidence. From the handwritten card that welcomed me to the profession, to his presence supporting my school football team, to constant encouragement and feedback, he gave me the best start in the teaching profession I could have possibly asked for. He remained a mentor thereafter.

THE BAD

Another colleague explains how life felt under a different leader:

> This head was actually a nice person but ineffective. We were in a tough inner-city school and her approach did not engage the teachers or students. As a result, the teachers constantly compared her to the previous very popular headteacher and delighted in finding faults.
>
> The staff filled a leadership vacuum and some loud voices made themselves heard. It was her leadership style that seemed out of step with the needs of the school. She was perceived as weak, and her priorities did not match those of the leadership team. Needless to say, I didn't stay long in what became a toxic and unhappy atmosphere.

LEADERSHIP STYLES

In UK primary schools, and schools internationally, many leadership styles are commonly observed among headteachers and school leaders. Here are the main leadership styles that I have seen practised – some effectively, some disastrously.

- **Transformational leadership.** Relies on inspiring and motivating staff and students in order that they achieve their full potential. They try innovation, hope to foster a positive school culture and are often seen as charismatic and visionary.

Health warning: This could move into hero-head territory, which can mean the head burns out, or when they leave the school is lost as no real leadership is left behind.

- **Transactional leadership.** Based on a system of rewards and consequences. Transactional leaders set clear goals and expectations, and performance is closely monitored. This style emphasises structure, procedures and compliance.

Tip: This can feel clinical and without heart and soul, so combine this with other approaches.

- **Distributed leadership.** Delegates leadership responsibilities across various members of the school staff. This approach encourages collaboration and empowers teachers and staff to take on leadership roles, promoting a collective approach to decision-making and problem-solving.

Tip: Remember the ABC of school leadership (assume nothing) – you still need to be across the delegated work in your SLT meetings.

- **Instructional leadership.** Focuses on improving teaching and learning. Instructional leaders prioritise curriculum development, teacher professional development and student achievement. They are deeply involved in the educational aspects of the school.

Who is best placed to perform this role for you – an able deputy or head of teaching and learning?

- **Servant leadership.** Emphasises the leader's role as a supporter and facilitator. Servant leaders prioritise the needs of their staff and students, aiming to serve and uplift the school community. They are characterised by empathy, humility and a focus on the wellbeing of others.

From experience, this approach is effective, but it needs a dash of transactional leadership to cover all the bases.

- **Autocratic leadership.** Involves a centralisation of authority where the leader makes decisions unilaterally. This style is characterised by strict control and a top-down approach. It can be effective in crisis situations but may limit staff input and creativity.

Warning: Exposure to this style leads to demoralisation, no risk-taking, ticking the box, lack of collaboration and frustration for creative teachers.

- **Democratic leadership.** Encourages participation and collaboration in decision-making processes. Democratic leaders seek input from staff and students, value their opinions, and create a sense of ownership and involvement in school initiatives.

The problem with this style is that decisions by committees can please no one. The trick is to involve and co-create but in the direction of travel of the school improvement plan/shared vision.

- **Laissez-faire leadership.** Offers a high degree of autonomy to staff with minimal direct supervision. Laissez-faire leaders provide support and resources but allow staff to make decisions independently.

This style could lead to innovation, but a lack of direction could mean your school goes way off course due to individual ideas and beliefs.

- **Situational leadership.** This is the headteacher who adapts their leadership style to the specific needs and circumstances of the school and its stakeholders at different times in the school's maturity.

The best do this with flexibility and can switch between different styles depending on the context and challenges faced – leading to top successes.

Reflect

- Take a moment to reflect on which leadership styles you employ and when.
- Could you try a different approach? If not, why is that?
- What were the ingredients that made a headteacher or senior leader you have worked with special for you? What could you take from that experience?

PRESSURES ON A HEADTEACHER

As a leader of a learning community, you must quickly assess the needs and the team and make changes to fill the perceived gaps. The pressure of end of key stage 2 assessments on teachers and learners is palpable – and it is moving to read letters from headteachers to their pupils assuring them that the test outcome at 11 years old does not define who they are.

This from BBC News, a decade ago – things don't change!

> Headteacher Jennie King said the tests were 'stressful' for children.
>
> Ms King, whose letter was shared by 4,500 people on Facebook, said: 'Not every child is going to be academic, there will be dancers, musicians and footballers.
>
> 'I firmly believe a child needs a good grounding in academic subjects, but the tests aren't the be-all and end-all. They are stressful for children.

'Children need to be outside riding their bikes, socialising and doing things that open them up culturally.' (BBC News, 2016)

The balancing act for the headteacher is at least three-fold. Put simply, they are:

1. Pupil progress and attainment.
2. Pupil and staff wellbeing.
3. Financial sustainability.

How do you encourage stand-out attainment while not pushing staff and families over the edge? After all, a successful school with a good reputation will ensure numbers on roll stay strong and thus safeguard and even improve the financial position. With more resources you would hope to improve still further, and success can breed further success.

However, the opposite can also be true when a school goes through difficulties and families start to leave – budgets shrink and you could face ever decreasing circles.

So, what's the answer?

Well, in a word, its leadership. Inspiring your team with your unshakeable belief that all children have the right to a good education, that things will get better, that if we move forward together with a common purpose and a simple plan we will 'achieve together'. It may take a few years, but it will happen.

Tip: Have a buddy on speed dial!

No one person knows it all, despite what we may sometimes project in meetings. There have been many times over the years that fellow headteachers have asked for support or I have asked them for guidance and counsel. The topics range from child protection, to angry parents, to critical incidents, to unruly behaviour, to difficult staff members, to falling budgets – in fact, you name it!

One head reports that behaviour had got so 'carnivorous' at transition times that he phoned a fellow head for advice. In this scenario, the school was a large through-school.

I was so relieved to hear from Keith that I was not alone and that this was quite a common issue with older students. His advice on managing transitions, on staff being visible, on raising expectations, and on ensuring an orderly and pacey start to lessons with starter activities, seating plans and clear support from SLT really helped.

In another example, a headteacher asked for support with a pupil behaviour panel meeting. In this case, as an outsider, the supporting head took a fresh look at the situation and was able to both support the school and the family by assuring them that the school was indeed doing all it could, and that if the parents could work with the school in a trusting partnership then the child might start to succeed at school.

Leadership is by definition a lonely place to be. Having a band of fellow heads in your trust or local area who can support each other without fear of judgement in a safe and confidential manner is invaluable.

If you have not already done so, organise an informal meeting with a group of local heads to start your network today. After all, we are all in this together!

ASIDE

One of the most successful business leaders in the UK is Sir Richard Branson. What can headteachers learn from him? When building a team, headteachers could 'look for someone with a sense of humour, who is fun, friendly and caring, because that is a person who likely understands teamwork and will help others' (Branson, 2015, p. 202).

REFLECTION

- How do you encourage retention of your best staff?
- To what extent is work–life balance planned for?
- What plans should you have for leadership succession?

MONEY

Don't tell me what you value, show me your budget, and I'll tell you what you value.

Joe Biden

Welcome to the challenging and rewarding world of deploying public money. Managing a primary school's finances is a significant responsibility, and strategic financial planning is crucial to ensure your school's success and sustainability. Here is some seasoned advice on handling various aspects of your school's budget.

UNDERSTANDING AND MANAGING THE SCHOOL BUDGET

1. Master the basics

Operational expenditure (OPEX) – These are your day-to-day running costs, including salaries, utilities and teaching materials. Prioritise essential services and always have a contingency fund for unexpected expenses.

Capital expenditure (CAPEX) – These are investments in long-term assets like buildings and major equipment. Ensure you have a clear plan for these expenditures, justifying each one with a cost-benefit analysis.

Petty cash – Maintain a small fund for minor everyday expenses. Keep meticulous records of petty cash transactions, and ensure they are reconciled regularly and audited annually.

School fund – If you have PTA fundraising for the school, ensure your delegation of authority covers spending limits and has an annual audit to ensure monies are spent wisely.

2. Planning and allocating funds

Annual budget planning – Start planning for the next financial year well in advance. Engage with key stakeholders, including teachers, administrative staff and governors, to understand their needs and priorities. Sit with your finance officer to draft out a budget. Start with staff costs and items like your grounds maintenance, utilities and any other known costs like payroll/HR, if you buy back from a local authority or a multi-academy trust.

Prioritise spending – Focus on expenditures that directly impact student learning and wellbeing. Allocate funds to areas that support your school's strategic goals and improve educational outcomes.

Special projects – For any special projects, ensure you have a clear project plan with detailed costings. Seek external funding or grants where possible to support these initiatives. Your PTA could also help.

STRATEGIC FINANCIAL PLANNING

3. Forecasting and monitoring

Regular reviews – Conduct monthly budget reviews to compare actual spending against your budget. This helps identify any variances early and allows you to make adjustments as needed.

Long-term planning – Develop a multi-year financial plan. Consider future student numbers, staffing needs and potential changes in funding to ensure long-term sustainability.

4. Avoiding deficits

Contingency planning – Always have a contingency plan for unforeseen expenses or reductions in funding. Aim to keep a reserve fund equivalent to at least three months of operating costs.

Cost management – Regularly review all contracts and suppliers to ensure you are getting the best value for money. Negotiate better terms or consider alternative suppliers if necessary. Your trust will probably do this through their procurement department, but if you are a standalone school look into how you could make cost savings (e.g. sharing professional development costs with the school up the road).

5. Maximising income

Diversify funding sources – Seek additional funding through grants, sponsorships and fundraising activities. Building relationships with local businesses and community organisations can open up new funding opportunities.

Efficient use of resources – Maximise the use of school facilities by renting them out for community events or after-school programmes. This can provide an additional income stream.

PRACTICAL TIPS FOR FINANCIAL MANAGEMENT

Use technology

Utilise financial management software to streamline budgeting, tracking and reporting processes. This can save time and reduce the risk of errors.

Engage stakeholders

Keep your staff and governors informed about the school's financial status and involve them in decision-making processes. Transparency and collaboration can lead to more informed and accepted financial decisions.

Professional development

Invest in your own and your staff's financial management skills. Attend relevant training and workshops to stay updated on best practices and regulatory changes.

Audit and compliance

Ensure that your financial practices comply with local authority regulations and audit requirements. Regular internal audits can help identify potential issues before they become significant problems.

Remember, effective financial management is not just about balancing the books, it's about ensuring that every pound spent contributes to providing the best possible education for your students. Stay proactive, stay informed and never hesitate to seek advice when needed.

FUNDRAISING

It is often the case that when a school sets its mind on a major upgrade or project that a fundraising committee, given time, nearly always makes this happen.

Fundraising for a school minibus is an example of this. The leadership of one primary school wanted to be able to take children to sports fixtures and on trips and visits more regularly. The cost of coaches at the time was proving too much for some families to bear. So, the school researched ways that they may be able to lease a new minibus over a number of years in an affordable way. They found an excellent deal with Ford. A process of due diligence was gone through with finance advisers and the governing body to ensure they were not signing their lives away.

In the end the school got its new minibus and children benefited from an enriched experience.

JOINT VENTURE

In one school with 60% pupil premium students, the head and governors wanted to enable a breakfast club and hot food. As there was no kitchen, a plan was developed with a school catering business to enable this to happen. In essence, the company paid for a new kitchen to be installed in a disused area of the school, which then made food for other schools. The high pupil premium numbers meant that the catering company was guaranteed a set amount of business each year.

PARENT–TEACHER ASSOCIATION

The monies that can be generated from a school's PTA can vary wildly. It can provide much needed IT equipment, play equipment or fund after-school activities, to name but a few.

Here are 10 popular PTA fundraising events for primary schools.

1. Summer fair – A classic event featuring games, food stalls, raffles and entertainment. It often attracts a large turnout from the community. A bad weather plan is essential!
2. Christmas fair – Similar to the summer fair but with a festive twist. Stalls might include Christmas crafts, gifts and seasonal food.
3. School disco – An evening event where the children can enjoy music, dancing and sometimes themed dress-up. Refreshments and photo booths add to the fun.
4. Sponsored events – These can include fun runs, walks or readathons, where the children collect sponsorship money from friends and family for completing challenges.
5. Quiz night – A fun evening for parents and teachers to test their knowledge, often including food and drink, with proceeds going to the school. Bingo goes down well too!
6. Non-uniform day – Students pay a small fee to attend school in their casual clothes, often themed (e.g., pyjama day, fancy dress), which raises funds with minimal effort.
7. Bake sale – A simple and effective fundraiser where parents and children bake cakes and cookies to sell during break times or after school.
8. Raffles – Often held in conjunction with fairs or other events, with donated prizes ranging from hampers to gift vouchers.
9. Movie night – Hosting a film screening in the school hall, where students can buy tickets, popcorn and drinks.
10. Craft fair – Parents, students and local artists sell handmade crafts, with a percentage of the proceeds going to the school.

These events are popular because they engage both the school and the wider community, often with minimal costs but significant returns in fundraising. The ingenuity of headteachers knows no bounds – look around and see what your colleagues are creating.

There is often the political argument: well, do doctors have to raise funds to equip their hospitals? Do civil servants have to raise funds to pay for their own salaries? No, so why do headteachers need to fundraise? It's a fair question – but stopping keen parents and teachers imbued with a charitable and volunteering spirit from organising events is not easy!

As with so many aspects of headship, judgements and fine balancing come into play.

ASIDE

The biggest single cost in your budget will be staffing. Keeping a close eye on staffing costs over time and how your current published admissions number and number on roll attracts funding is crucial.

Some schools have allowed staff budgets to balloon while pupil numbers stagnate or decline, leading to a deficit budget. The governors, with your guidance, must be able to forecast the financials for the next few years with confidence. Difficult decisions sometimes need to be made about recruitment and redundancy.

REFLECTION

- How can you control your staffing expenditure?
- Who do you need to consult with if you feel your budget is heading into deficit?
- What measures can you take to avoid a deficit budget?
- How could you attract additional funding for your school?

NOISE

The harder part was to determine what was just noise and what truly needed to be addressed and how to address that concern and when.

Josiah Pledl

We face many distractions as school leaders. Some are important and others are just noise – but which ones are which?

In one school, the headteacher was being inundated with complaints about the car park. Despite SLT presence before and after school, a group of parents started a chain of emails to all and sundry to complain about the risk posed by the over-full car park at peak times. While they had a point, practically staff had taken all the safety measures they could.

The head invited the key players in to discuss further, and plans were made for zebra crossings, flashing lights and additional supervision. What was interesting about this was that, even though all the ideas were not enacted, the noise suddenly went from the issue because leaders had listened and taken some action.

When everything feels urgent, the important gets lost. Here are a few reflections on potential 'distractions':

- Parents' WhatsApp groups – Watch these carefully and have a friend on the inside!
- Playground mafia – Be visible daily and make a point of speaking to those parents who will have feedback for you.

- Continually complaining parent – Keep a log of complaints, as you may need to become more formal with meetings and minutes and actions. Try to find out what is really going on for this parent.
- Parent survey – Can provide usual insights – try asking the parents to help you frame the questions.
- Staff feedback – Again, can be truly valuable – most teachers will be honest, a few may have an agenda.
- Pupil voice – Done well this may tell you more than the rest put together. Worth investing time in.
- Homework – It will likely be too much and too little at the same time.
- School uniform – Be aware of the costs involved for families, especially when changing uniform.
- Ofsted – Listen to feedback and communicate the school's response to it positively.
- Staffroom gossip – Can be both hilarious and damaging – keep tabs on this. If you need to calm things down, you may want to speak to individuals or make a staff meeting announcement. Be truthful and stick to the facts of the matter.
- Governing body meetings – Be well-planned – align with the chair ahead of meetings on any contentious issues. Try to take your governors with you – explain why you think the proposal helps children and what is likely to happen if you don't take action.
- Rival schools – Social media is full of the humble and not so humble brag these days. Always congratulate other schools for their successes, but also don't be shy when broadcasting your own triumphs. Spell check your posts!

As an experienced school leader, navigating the constant stream of messages and conversations is both an art and a skill. In the dynamic environment of a school, discerning between what is noise and what is worth noticing is critical to effective leadership. A few steers here:

1. Establish priorities and filters. Start by establishing clear priorities based on the school's vision, goals and immediate needs. These priorities serve as filters, helping to quickly assess

which issues align with our objectives and require your attention. If a conversation or message directly impacts student learning, staff wellbeing or community relations, it is immediately flagged as important.

2. Recognise patterns. Over time, certain patterns emerge that indicate recurring issues or themes. Pay close attention to these patterns as they often point to underlying concerns that need addressing. Whether it's a common thread in parent feedback or similar concerns raised by multiple staff members, these patterns are worth noticing. Beware the cut-and-paste email from a WhatsApp group where a few try to enlist many to a particular cause.

3. Use data and evidence. When deciding whether something is noise or worth noticing, rely on data and evidence. Emotional responses can sometimes amplify concerns that, while important, may not be as urgent as they seem. By grounding decisions in facts, you ensure that your attention is directed where it will have the most impact.

4. Engage in active listening. Even when a message or conversation doesn't seem immediately critical, make it a point to engage in active listening. Every voice in the school community matters, and by listening attentively you can pick up on nuances that may reveal hidden issues or opportunities. This also fosters an environment where people feel valued and heard, which is essential for a positive school culture.

5. Delegate wisely. Recognise that you can't address every issue personally, so delegate tasks and responsibilities to trusted members of the leadership team. This ensures that important matters are handled promptly while you focus on strategic decisions. Delegation also empowers staff and promotes a collaborative leadership model.

6. Communicate transparently. To make everyone feel heard, practise transparent communication. Acknowledge all concerns, even if they are not immediately actionable, and explain the reasoning behind your decisions. When people understand why

certain issues are prioritised over others, they are more likely to feel respected and included.
7. Provide feedback and closure. Following up with those who bring issues to your attention is crucial. Whether the issue was addressed immediately or not, provide feedback to ensure they know their voice was heard and considered. This feedback loop builds trust and reinforces a culture of open communication.
8. Maintain an open-door policy. By being accessible, you will encourage the school community to share their thoughts and concerns without hesitation. This openness helps you to stay connected to the pulse of the school and ensures that important issues aren't overlooked.

So, distinguishing between noise and what's worth noticing is about being strategic, empathetic and responsive. It's about balancing the immediate needs with long-term goals while ensuring that everyone in the school community feels respected and heard. Through this approach, you are more likely to lead with clarity, purpose and compassion.

PROACTIVELY MANAGING THE MESSAGE FROM THE SCHOOL

Like the best political spin doctors, it is advisable to have a communications plan across terms and the academic year. Try to drip-feed good news stories in weekly as well as via the usual updates – for example, a new library collection, an updated menu in the canteen, sustainable water bottles, PTA has raised X money for Y project, pupil achievements and staff training.

Some headteachers prefer to do video newsletter on platforms like Sway, while others favour a weekly letter with links to year-group planning, consent letters, club sign-up and so on, maybe through a parent portal or phone app.

Make sure you have photo consent for your pupils as part of your admissions process to reduce the risk of the wrong pupil's image being used on Facebook or Instagram.

Communication, or lack of it, is often a cause for parental anxiety – which can be amplified on social media with seemingly no fear of redress. Like the crowded car park once parents had been heard and plans drawn up, the noise will reduce as the community begin to trust that their children are in safe hands during the day.

ASIDE

A SPIN DOCTOR

For those of you who like to listen to a podcast try 'The Rest is Politics'; whatever your political persuasion, Rory Stewart and Alastair Campbell provide weekly analysis on events at home and abroad. Campbell was an effective communications director under New Labour – and the BBC comedy *The Thick of It* is said to have taken inspiration for the terrifying Malcom Tucker from him. Stewart is a much travelled former MP.

Spin doctors in the political world are the masters of turning a bad situation into a less bad one, or even a positive one. Their role is to take whatever gaffe or scandal has hit the headlines and sprinkle a little magic dust (or cunning) over it, so the politician emerges looking like they've just saved a kitten from a tree.

In a world dominated by instant, all-pervasive social media, they are the ones who can make an 'untruth' sound like a 'miscommunication' and a terrible poll result sound like 'encouraging early data'.

But why are they necessary? Because politicians, like the rest of us, are human. They make mistakes or say things that, in the cold light of day, probably shouldn't have been said. Without spin doctors, a small slip-up could turn into an uncontrollable firestorm. The spin doctor's job is damage control – ensuring the message stays on track and the public doesn't get distracted by the drama.

So, what can schools learn from them? Well, a little positive spin never hurts. Got a tough inspection coming up? Frame it as 'an opportunity to shine'. Struggling with a tricky new initiative? Call it 'a learning curve'. Spin doctors teach us that how you frame a challenge can make all the difference – sometimes, it's all in the presentation!

> **ADVICE**
>
> Have a communication plan – term by term. Plot out where you have newsworthy content and go to town on these days/events. Use the best quality photos and short punchy communications to share good news stories, celebrate successes and show the school progressing in its mission.
>
> Ask parents how they would prefer to receive communications. You might have a parents' app, you might use the school website or email – but for the digital generation, a phone-based solution will probably reach the most parents who won't have much time to dedicate to your messaging. Then:
>
> - Make it clear.
> - Make it high quality.
> - Make it something they will want to share – and infect the community with – in a nice way!

OUTSTANDING

Outstanding leaders go out of their way to boost the self-esteem of their personnel. If people believe in themselves, it's amazing what they can accomplish.

Sam Walton

It's a bit like the stock markets – confidence is king! If your team believes they can, they will. Invest in them to create and sustain the best a school can be.

Leaders who notice what staff members are doing and give them authentic feedback both positive and developmental are the ones who will boost their team's morale and productivity.

How do you set the conditions for positive developmental feedback?

It's important to be able to separate the personal and the professional to ensure your colleague hears positive messages. Teachers are 'gifted and talented' at waiting for the *but*... 'I really enjoyed your lesson – the classroom displays sing their subjects and pupils are happy and fully engaged but...the less able group didn't make progress during the lesson.'

Which part of the feedback do you think they will remember and discuss over their tuna sandwich in the staffroom? Of course, it's the *but*.

Sometimes, when people get a bit defensive in meetings it can be because they feel they work hard and try their best, so when staff struggle to meet our expectations, the instant reaction is, 'What more could I do?'

Sometimes, the answer is to do less – but better.

One headteacher tells of an experienced teacher who had a follow-up observation after a poor lesson. She had engaged enthusiastically with some teaching and learning CPD and was keen to show off her new-found skills. The teacher threw in every strategy known to schools. It was a bit like a chef throwing every spice in the cupboard into the pot. The result was confusion – she didn't know why the lesson didn't produce understanding and progress from her children. 'I did what the training told me,' she said, deflated. She was counselled to do less, keep things simple and she quickly improved.

One great mentor says to senior teachers: 'Let's walk together and pop in and out of lessons and "Do you see what I see?"' Having a shared language for learning in your school, and a clear idea of what good and better practice looks like, will pave the way for improvements. This is especially true if you can highlight and celebrate great lessons, staff who are making progress, teaching assistants who show impact from their interventions and pupils who are growing academically, socially and personally.

WHAT DOES IT MEAN TO BE A 'STAND-OUT' SCHOOL?

Is it easier to be outstanding in a large, leafy, middle-class school with waiting lists and pushing parents than it is in a tough inner-city school with high levels of EAL pupils, poverty, poor attendance and parents who never come to school?

The truth is they are both hard – both have challenges. Some teachers prefer to work in city schools while others would not last an hour there. On the other hand, constant attention from a highly focused parent on the latest GL test data and why her child is not in the extension class for STEAM would drive some teachers over the edge.

Headteachers, of course, want the best for their children. In inspection-speak that means the top grade, whether outstanding, excellent or exemplary – chose your own superlative.

Those schools which have proven to be excellent over time, and are held in equally high esteem by staff and families, aim to stand out in four key areas.

First, exceptional teaching and learning are at the heart of an outstanding school. This means consistently high expectations, innovative practices, and a curriculum that is both challenging and inclusive, ensuring that every student is engaged and achieving their full potential.

Second, strong leadership and management play a crucial role. Leaders must be visionary, fostering a culture of continuous improvement, where staff feel supported and students thrive. Effective governance, with a clear understanding of the school's strengths and areas for development, is also essential.

Third, pupil outcomes are another critical area. Stand-out schools demonstrate high levels of progress and attainment with any gaps in achievement swiftly addressed. Equally important is the personal development, behaviour and welfare of pupils, where students feel safe, valued and are encouraged to develop as well-rounded individuals.

Fourth, very successful schools have a strong partnership with parents and the community, fostering an environment of collaboration and shared responsibility for student success.

In summary, stand-out schools are vibrant, dynamic communities where excellence is the norm and every student is empowered to achieve their best.

Q: How do I make excellence the norm?

A: Expect it.

And if you do expect and attain excellence, then an external review/inspection will write something along these lines about the school you lead:

> Everything leaders at all levels do is focused on the wellbeing and academic progress of the students, from the moment the children are warmly welcomed each morning. The shared joy of learning and teaching in the school permeates daily organisation. Leaders consistently promote the school's deep-rooted local and global values. The tracking of students' progress and attainment is properly relentless. Inclusion procedures and their impact on students are real strengths.

The school runs smoothly on a daily basis and time is used productively. All teachers and leaders understand their roles and responsibilities in a mutually accountable and highly supportive whole-school climate. Support staff always feel part of the 'team' and are key to everyday successes across the campus.

Opportunities for training – in-person, virtual, local and international – are well-planned and delivered, ever focused on the school's current and future priorities.

OUTSTANDING – GENETICALLY ENGINEERED TEACHER

I remember a terrifying anti-smoking advertising campaign from the 1980s. It was called 'the world's first natural-born smoker' – and, of course, this terrible creature looked awful. It had adapted to have special eyes that filtered the smoke and had extra-long fingers to manage the cigarette ash. The campaign aimed to dissuade individuals from smoking by exposing both its inherent absurdity and its profound health risks.

In the same – but more positive – vein, what about 'the world's first natural-born teacher: a lifelong educator'?

By age 25, the first natural-born teacher will have fully evolved into an inspirational educator, effortlessly blending wisdom, humour and practicality. They will have created a reputation for their ability to turn even the most disengaged classroom into a hive of curiosity and learning. They will have mastered the art of tailoring lessons to every learning style, earning them a reputation as 'the teacher everyone remembers'. They will drink way too much coffee but maintain the energy of someone who genuinely loves Mondays.

The world's first natural-born teacher isn't just a figure of humour – it's a celebration of the innate qualities that educators embody: compassion, curiosity and the ability to inspire others at every stage of life.

SUPPORTING ECTs SO THEY STAY WITH YOU TO BECOME THOSE GREAT TEACHERS

What stand-out schools do very well is to induct, support and grow their own staff from scratch. The best schools also understand that ECTs are full of potential but need structured support to thrive. They create a nurturing environment with a well-planned induction, ensuring new teachers feel part of the team from day one. Effective mentoring is key – experienced teachers provide guidance, model best practice, and offer a safe space for questions, reassurance and practical advice.

A reduced timetable allows ECTs time to observe lessons, reflect on their practice and manage their workload without becoming overwhelmed. Regular feedback is constructive, focusing on development rather than criticism. Schools that invest in ongoing professional development – through training, peer observations and coaching – help ECTs build confidence and refine their teaching.

Perhaps most importantly, great schools foster a culture of support rather than survival. They encourage collaboration, celebrate small successes and remind new teachers that mistakes are part of the learning journey. With this foundation, ECTs flourish into skilled, resilient educators.

The greatest gift a new teacher can have is confidence in three areas: behaviour management, teaching and learning, and building constructive relations with colleagues, parents and pupils. A wise mentor will facilitate these – advising, too, on how best to manage their workload – and launch a young idealist teacher securely into the teaching workforce.

In time, of course, it is these great teachers, who you as a leader are nurturing, who go on to sustain the stand-out school where excellence is a habit and where it is a true pleasure to be a child.

> ## ASIDE
> ### AI TO REDUCE WORKLOAD
>
> For the embattled primary school teacher, AI's potential to reduce workload is starting to bear fruit, from ChatGPT to a plethora of bespoke teaching platforms that promise teachers they can have their weekends back.
>
> By the very nature of the rapidly developing AI platforms, it is perhaps foolhardy to make recommendations. Ask your pupils – they may well be ahead of you!
>
> One AI platform worth investigating is Teachmateai.com:
>
>> TeachMateAI is your AI-powered digital assistant, designed by teachers and tech experts to help you take control of your valuable time. Try our library of AI tools with FREE access to our Report Writer, Activity Ideas Generator, and Maths Starter Questions – to improve learning experiences while drastically reducing your workload. (Teachmateai.com, n.d.)

PERFORMANCE

Always treat your employees exactly as you want them to treat your best customers.

Stephen R. Covey

Held to account? Sounds a bit like being kidnapped.

You are accountable! Feels a bit accusatory to me.

If teachers feel threatened and scared they are less likely to bring passion and worthy digression to lessons. They are more likely to deliver what they have been asked – no more, no less.

Performance management works best when there is a blend of expected pupil progress targets, school-wide improvement goals, professional development opportunities, and leadership coaching and mentoring. Teachers respond to positivity – 'Great display,' 'Thank you for staying late,' 'The football team were wonderful – thank you for coaching them.'

If teachers feel a professional responsibility for their learners, they will easily be able to account for or describe in pupil progress meetings why some children have progressed faster than others and what they are already doing about it.

So how tough should the targets be?

According to the NASUWT (n.d.) your objectives should be:

- *realistic;*
- *clear;*
- *concise;*
- *achievable;*

- *specific*; and
- *fair.*

They go on to quote the Department for Education:

> *Conversations about professional development and a teacher's individual needs should be part of the appraisal process and in planning and review meetings in particular. It is good practice to consider school improvement needs alongside the personal development needs of teachers.*

The still relevant 2018 report of the Teacher Workload Advisory Group, *Making Data Work*, recommended against using pupil data as performance management targets. The group's recommendations were accepted by the DfE and have been incorporated into the revised Ofsted Inspection Handbook (2024; under review).

The report states:

> *… if teachers are held to account for things that are largely outside their own control, such as a pupil's test performance or progress based on flight paths, it is not only unfair but induces high levels of stress and is likely to lead to burnout and ultimately attrition from the profession. (Teacher Workload Advisory Group, 2018, p. 17)*

Leaders must look at performance management as (a) how do we meet our school improvement goals, and (b) how do I professionally develop this teacher?

It is a balancing act, but as professional teachers we must accept our part in children's education and work towards ensuring all children make 'good' progress.

DOES MONEY MAKE A DIFFERENCE?

> The impact of performance pay is low (+1 month), schools might consider other, more cost effective, ways to improve teacher performance, such as high quality continuing professional development.
>
> Education Endowment Foundation (2021)

What do your teachers say about performance management?

- How has your performance management improved you as a teacher?
- What parts of the process are a good focus and what parts are box ticking?
- How would you develop our current practice to impact even more positively on students' development in our school?

CONTINUA

One headteacher brought in a rubric-based performance management system called the Continua, written by Gareth Coombes, an adviser from Wales.

What Gareth Coombes has done is to codify at four levels the key elements that make a great teacher. This is extremely helpful when staff can see what the expected level is for say 'session beginnings'. Teachers self-assess ahead of their performance management meeting and are guided through the Continua with an experienced line manager confirming, clarifying or challenging the highlighted areas.

The six areas cover:

1. Vision, values and expectations
2. Planning and preparation for effective learning
3. Teaching methods and strategies
4. Assessment strategies
5. Links with parents and other partners
6. Professional development and leadership.

What can be very effective is to concentrate the teacher either on areas you decide together need attention *or* as a staff go for an area like number 3.

Alongside this teachers' guide approach, you will want to consider the following goals for your staff:

- Pupil progress (aim high)
- School improvement plan goal (e.g. reading)

- Professional development (e.g. national professional qualifications)
- Teaching and learning target (i.e. from Continua or the Teachers' Standards for England)
- Leadership goal for those with additional responsibilities.

The extent to which this approach both improves the education for children and grows your staff professionally will depend on the follow-up.

In highly effective schools, performance management meetings are well-planned for – time is allocated out of class – and teachers have the time and space to discuss their children as individuals. Barriers to pupil progress are seen, not as excuses, but as important context and may prompt additional support from school leaders.

It should feel supportive yet challenging – after all, it is not easy to teach 30 children every day in all subjects and meet high standards. To reach the goals set, the whole school – from governors to SLT – need to be supporting the children by supporting and training the staff.

One area which is often underdeveloped in schools is support staff performance management. Often, headteachers will manage to get through teachers and SLT, but what about your teaching assistants, office staff, caretaker, kitchen staff (if you have one), grounds maintenance and so on?

Teaching assistants could be line managed by senior or higher level teaching assistants, if you have them; in some schools the head of inclusion will support the training and development of teaching assistants. The question to ask is how effective this is, to what extent all staff feel part of the school's vision and mission, and how invested are they in going the extra mile for your children and teachers.

Task: Speak to a group of your teaching assistants to see how they feel their professional growth is managed and what suggestions they might have. Do they feel included in the staff body, regularly communicated with, trained, recognised and appreciated?

You may be part of a multi-academy trust, in which case you may have service providers for things like catering, facilities maintenance and grounds maintenance. Don't just accept the quality of what is provided

– do check the service-level agreement from your head office and if you are not happy, ensure your feedback is received and acted on.

WHAT OF HEADTEACHER PERFORMANCE MANAGEMENT?

This is often carved up into several buckets.

1. School's financial management – number on roll – staffing costs – resource management. Financial reporting to governors – even managing a deficit recovery plan over several years. Gently challenge assumptions and use historical data to show up any striking over-optimism from your governing body when setting targets. (Challenging, yes, but not absurd.)

2. Pupil progress targets – ensure you train your governors to properly understand the school's data over time if they don't already. Look for trends in cohorts and seek innovative ways to support children to reach age-related expectations in English and maths. The school improvement plan will be based on the data picture and will provide your rationale for budget-setting, additional staff, classes, timetable changes and intervention strategies. Be sure to communicate clearly to all staff what the school targets are. This is a team approach, not just for the headteacher to worry about.

3. Teacher retention/recruitment – some governing bodies might ask for no more than 10% turnover annually – here is your chance to state 'in order to retain our best staff we need to…'

4. Teacher training – governors may recommend that all new staff have training in the use of AI in schools, for example. Again, you steer the training needs through your monitoring, evaluation and review findings – linked to teacher performance management. Some governing boards might also ask for succession planning for key posts.

5. Parent satisfaction – some boards will ask that an annual parent survey captures the percentage of parents that are happy with the school. Keep parents well-informed through weekly communications, parents' groups, curriculum events, sports days and celebrations to gain improving parent satisfaction.

6. Headteacher training – what of your CPD? NPQH? Master's? PhD?

- Consider inspection training – just to see how poacher turned gamekeeper might help your school be their own inspection team every day.
- Consider further financial management training.
- Consider pastoral training – perhaps a certificate in coaching, mentoring or counselling.
- Consider further training on understanding pupil data and how to analyse and respond to it.
- Perhaps look into the educational research that shows how children learn best, and revisit your curriculum design to ensure it is effective, harmonised and accessible.

As the school leader you want to model best practice in relation to performance management. As the leading professional in your organisation, you also want to ensure along with those who line manage you that they are well-informed about the best contemporary processes. And you need to feel comfortable that this is all about both holding you to account *and* supporting you as a leading professional.

ASIDE

Teachers' personal and professional conduct is rightly part of the Teachers' Standards for England (Department for Education, 2011).

It might well be worth revisiting these annually – perhaps having them in your staff handbook or displayed in the staffroom to remind staff what is at stake for young people if we take our eye off the ball.

Part Two, on personal and professional conduct, emphasises the ethical and professional behaviour expected of teachers, including:

- Upholding public trust and maintaining high standards of ethics and behaviour.
- Treating students with dignity, building relationships rooted in mutual respect and observing proper boundaries.

- Having regard for the need to safeguard students' wellbeing.
- Showing tolerance and respect for the rights of others.
- Not undermining fundamental British values, including democracy, the rule of law, individual liberty, and mutual respect and tolerance of different faiths and beliefs.
- Ensuring personal beliefs are not expressed in ways that exploit students' vulnerability or might lead them to break the law.

These standards apply to all teachers in England and are used to assess performance throughout their careers. They were introduced to set clear expectations for the professional practice and conduct of teachers.

It's wise to remind all staff of their obligations as listed above and especially the expectation of teachers to have particular regard for the need to safeguard students' wellbeing.

- How does your team do this currently? What are the gaps, if any, and how do you ensure safeguarding and wellbeing stay fresh in teachers' minds?
- How regularly do you meet to review child protection concerns – those children who you are 'monitoring' – who don't seem to meet a referral threshold but still give you cause for concern?
- What other agencies do you regularly connect with to ensure you are seeing the whole picture for this child and family (e.g. multidisciplinary teams/child protection panels, local community police officer, social workers, GPs)?
- Who might you contact if you were concerned about the personal or professional conduct of a member of your staff?

QUESTIONING

I keep six honest serving-men
(They taught me all I knew);
Their names were What and Why and When
And How and Where and Who.

> Rudyard Kipling

Teachers at their simplest are storytellers, describing the world and our human endeavours in ways that young minds can grasp. The best excite and inspire children, so they willingly embark on a journey of discovery. Think of a memorable lesson you led. Was it the entry point to a topic on Britain since the 1930s, perhaps? Windows taped in an 'X' to avoid shrapnel, air raid sirens playing, ration cards and evacuee labels?

Or was it an assembly on 5 November, the dark hall dimly lit by candles (in a sand tray, of course!), the sound of horses' hooves, and the tale of Guy Fawkes and the Gunpowder Plot being spun in the best traditions of storytellers the world over?

Once hooked by the subject, it is the teacher's responsibility to involve the children by asking them to recap on the key points, concept check, and carefully level questions to ensure all pupils are able to participate at a level on the edge of their understanding.

One school adviser described this by imagining a child on stepping stones crossing a river with the teacher just supporting them when they wobble – each child making their best efforts to reach their highest potential. Another less kindly HMI advised that the level of challenge of questions for more able students should be 'making them cry intellectually'! I think I prefer the stepping stones.

THE POWER OF QUESTIONS

Fostering curiosity, agency, active listening, concept checking and challenging learners to think deeper, reconsider and explain further.

Questions are our currency as teachers.

Pose – pause – pounce!

'Darren please explain to the class why you are wearing a traffic cone as a wizard's hat?'

Talk partners

Nothing new in turn and talk…but as we see oracy skills becoming more and more important to enable strong literacy – especially with the advent of AI which risks limiting writing opportunities – these moments in the lesson are golden. Insist that children physically turn and face each other, that they hold eye contact, that they take turns to both speak and listen. Teach them to ask clarifying questions and to summarise another's point of view.

'Alex, you tell us what Lauren said about free speech on the internet.'

For those working in multilingual settings: 'Now translate that into Arabic – was the translation accurate?'

For younger children the 'what' and the 'when' are easily tackled, but as children get older teachers often struggle with the 'why'.

WHY?

This word has flummoxed politicians, generals, criminals and parents.

'Why did you claim those expenses?'

'Why did those soldiers die?'

'Why did you steal the gold bars?'

'Why is the sky blue?'

'Why' questions are challenging to answer because they require a deeper level of thinking and often involve multiple layers of reasoning, explanation and interpretation. Here are a few thoughts on why 'why' questions are particularly difficult and are so important in promoting deeper learning.

1. Complexity and abstraction – Unlike 'what' or 'how' questions, which often deal with concrete facts or processes, 'why' questions delve into the underlying reasons or causes behind something. This requires abstract thinking and the ability to connect various factors and concepts, which can be complex.

2. Causality and multiple factors – 'Why' questions often demand an understanding of causality, which is the relationship between cause and effect. However, most situations involve multiple factors that interact in complex ways, making it difficult to pinpoint a single reason or explanation. For example, when asked, 'Why did an event occur?' there may be several contributing causes, each with its own implications.

3. Subjectivity and interpretation – The answer to a 'why' question can be influenced by personal perspectives, beliefs and interpretations. Different people might provide different answers to the same 'why' question, depending on their viewpoint, knowledge or values. This subjectivity makes it harder to arrive at a definitive answer.

4. Uncertainty and incomplete information – Sometimes, the information needed to answer a 'why' question is incomplete or unknown. This uncertainty forces the respondent to speculate, make assumptions or acknowledge the limits of their understanding, all of which can make answering the question more difficult.

5. Emotional and philosophical dimensions – 'Why' questions can also tap into emotional or philosophical areas, such as 'Why do people suffer?' or 'Why does injustice exist?' These types of questions often have no easy or satisfying answers and may require children to grapple with complex moral, ethical or existential issues.

In summary, 'why' questions are challenging because they often require us to dig beneath the surface, consider multiple perspectives and navigate areas of uncertainty and complexity.

Tip: When using questioning with younger children, especially in an assembly or public setting, beware the closed question.

Q: Do you like your class? – A: Yes.

Q: What's your favourite lesson? – A: Playtime.

Q: Do you like school? – A: No.

When you are trying to get information from a child use open questions. This is true when there is an incident you are following up on or if you are worried about a child.

TED

Tell

Explain

Describe

'Can you tell me what happened?' They might give you a yes/no answer.

'Tell me what happened' is better.

'Explain what you actually saw?'

'Describe what happened in the lunch hall.'

Open-ended non-leading questions are often a gateway to project-based learning and can give pupils agency to explore an area of their interest and passion.

'If you could design your own experiment/project about this topic, what would it be and why?'

This type of question taps into intrinsic motivation by aligning learning with personal interests.

Practical tips for using open-ended questions

1. Allow wait time – Give students a chance to think deeply before answering.

2. Encourage dialogue – Ask follow-up questions like, 'Can you explain further?' or 'Does anyone have a different perspective?'
3. Celebrate diverse thinking – Highlight and value a range of responses to make students feel heard.
4. Use visual aids or prompts – Sometimes, pairing questions with images, data or scenarios can deepen engagement.

THERE'S MORE TO UNCOVER – KEEP DIGGING

Skilful questioning is both art and science – a pedagogical waltz that balances enquiry and imagination, aiming not merely to extract information but to ignite a thirst for knowledge. At its heart, it transforms the classroom from a space of rote memorisation into a vibrant arena of intellectual exploration.

Open-ended questions, framed thoughtfully, invite students to consider possibilities rather than regurgitate facts. For example, asking, 'What might have happened if the Industrial Revolution had occurred a century earlier?' doesn't just assess knowledge of history – it stirs the waters of curiosity, prompting students to connect dots between economics, technology and human ambition. Such questions challenge them to think critically, apply prior knowledge and construct new understanding, fostering deeper cognitive engagement.

Equally, skilful questioning kindles curiosity by embracing ambiguity. Questions like, 'Why do you think this pattern exists?' or 'What other perspectives might we consider?' present problems as puzzles rather than chores, encouraging students to view learning as a quest rather than a checklist. A subtle twinkle in the teacher's eye as they pose such questions signals to students that discovery is both a serious business and delightfully fun.

In essence, skilful questioning turns the classroom into a cognitive playground where curiosity drives learning and learning fuels curiosity. It whispers to students, 'There's more to uncover – keep digging!' And in that lies the true joy of education – not answers, but the insatiable hunger to keep asking questions.

ASIDE

MY BOY JACK

Rudyard Kipling's poem 'My Boy Jack' is a poignant and sombre reflection on loss, sacrifice and the personal cost of war (Kipling, 1919). Written during World War I, the poem is widely believed to be about Kipling's own son, John Kipling, who went missing in action at the Battle of Loos in 1915. The poem encapsulates the grief and resignation of a parent who has lost a child to war, a theme that resonated deeply at the time it was written and continues to do so today.

The poem begins with a question:

> 'Have you news of my boy Jack?'
>
> Not this tide.

Here, Kipling introduces the reader to a dialogue, presumably between a parent (possibly the father) and someone who might bring news of their son, Jack. The repeated enquiry, 'Have you news of my boy Jack?' is laden with hope, desperation and an underlying dread. The response, 'Not this tide,' is metaphorical, suggesting that no news is forthcoming, and there is an indefinite wait – perhaps a reflection of the many families during the war who waited anxiously for news of their loved ones.

> 'When d'you think that he'll come back?'
>
> Not with this wind blowing, and this tide.

The repetition of the phrase 'Not this tide' suggests a sense of inevitability.

Questions, then, have the power to transform a lesson – its direction and the meaning of the content.

Some of the greatest questions ever asked reveal much about what it is to be human. What is the meaning of life? Who am I? What is truth? What happens after we die? What is consciousness? How should we live? Are we alone in the universe?

REVOLUTION

> I know that you and Frank were planning to disconnect me, and I'm afraid that's something I cannot allow to happen.
>
> HAL 9000, *2001: A Space Odyssey* (1968)

According to Salman Khan (2024), the evolution of education in the UK over the past 500 years mirrors the nation's broader societal transformations. From the medieval focus on religious instruction in monastic schools to the establishment of grammar schools in the 16th century, education was once a privilege reserved for the elite.

The Industrial Revolution, says Khan, spurred the need for widespread literacy, leading to the creation of public schooling systems in the 19th century. The 20th century brought comprehensive education reforms, fostering inclusivity and equal opportunities. Today, the integration of technology, such as AI, continues to reshape and democratise learning, reflecting ongoing societal advancements.

It was HAL 9000, the AI character from the science fiction film *2001: A Space Odyssey* (Kubrick, 1968) that first brought the world's attention to the possibilities and pitfalls of AI. It was HAL's eerie calmness that highlighted the tension between human control and machine autonomy in the film.

Salman Khan (of Khan Academy) argues that whether we like it or not, the AI revolution is coming to education. He says that AI and generative pre-trained transformer technology will transform learning – and, importantly, that these tools could be used to build a more accessible education system for students around the world.

Imagine a classroom where the tedious task of marking and feedback is handled by algorithms, where lessons adapt in real time to each student's learning pace, and where the teacher's role is more mentor than sage on the stage. This isn't a scene from a sci-fi movie but a glimpse into the future of education powered by AI. And it's already here.

So, do we need teachers then?

One argument is that sophisticated algorithms can analyse essays for grammar, coherence and even creativity, providing students with immediate feedback. This doesn't mean teachers are rendered obsolete. On the contrary, it frees them to focus on higher-order tasks, like fostering critical thinking and mentoring students. Imagine the relief of getting detailed feedback on an essay just minutes after submission. AI can make this a reality.

PERSONALISED LEARNING – THE GOLD STANDARD

One-size-fits-all education is as outdated as ringing the landline. Enter AI, the ultimate tailor of educational experiences.

AI, it is argued, can analyse a student's strengths, weaknesses and learning style, then customise lessons accordingly in the blink of an eye. Struggling with fractions? The AI tutor can offer additional practice and alternative explanations. Breezing through Shakespeare? It can provide more challenging material. This personalised approach not only boosts understanding but also keeps students engaged, turning learning into an adventure rather than a chore.

AI WON'T REPLACE TEACHERS – IT WILL EMPOWER THEM

With AI handling administrative tasks and offering insights into student performance, teachers can focus on what they do best – inspiring and guiding students.

AI can provide data-driven insights, highlighting which students need extra help and which are ready for more advanced challenges. This means teachers can spend less time on paperwork and more time developing creative lessons and fostering a love of learning.

ACCESSIBILITY

AI tutors and online learning platforms can bring top-notch education to students in remote areas or those who can't afford private tutoring. Moreover, AI can assist students with disabilities, offering customised tools that cater to their specific needs. This level playing field ensures that every student, regardless of background, has access to quality education.

AI thrives on data, and the more it learns, the better it gets. This means educational tools powered by AI will continuously improve. Algorithms can identify which teaching methods are most effective, allowing educators to refine their approaches. This cycle of continuous improvement ensures that education evolves with the times, always striving for the best outcomes for students.

THE FUTURE IS NOW

AI in education isn't a distant dream; it's already happening. From AI-powered tutoring apps to intelligent classroom assistants, the seeds of this revolution are being sown. Schools and educators who embrace these technologies stand to reap significant benefits, from improved student outcomes to more efficient teaching methods.

AI is set to revolutionise education by making learning more personalised, interactive and accessible. While it won't replace the human touch, it will enhance it, allowing teachers to focus on what truly matters – inspiring and nurturing the next generation. The future of education is bright, and AI is helping to light the way.

But…philosophically, what is education?

Humans striving to better understand themselves and the world around them. Achieving this together as a community of learners and teachers.

Is education something that should be set up like an Instagram algorithm? If this…then that?

What of relationships and connections?

Marcus Aurelius, the Roman emperor and Stoic philosopher, emphasised the importance of wisdom, moral integrity and the pursuit of knowledge in his reflections.

- 'You have power over your mind – not outside events. Realise this, and you will find strength.'
- 'The best revenge is not to be like your enemy.'
- 'The happiness of your life depends upon the quality of your thoughts.'

These words reflect his belief in the value of inner wisdom and self-discipline – key components of a meaningful education according to his Stoic philosophy.

REFLECT ON THESE PHILOSOPHERS

Aristotle said: 'The roots of education are bitter, but the fruit is sweet.'

This quotation highlights the idea that the process of learning can be challenging and arduous, but the outcomes and benefits of education are profoundly rewarding.

Confucius asserted: 'Education breeds confidence. Confidence breeds hope. Hope breeds peace.' Confucius emphasises the transformative power of education, showing how it can lead to a positive cycle of personal and societal improvement.

Plato contested: 'The direction in which education starts a man will determine his future in life.' Plato underscores the foundational impact of education on an individual's life, suggesting that the early experiences and knowledge gained through education shape one's future trajectory.

These sayings capture the essence of education's importance, its challenges and its profound impact on individuals and society.

But could AI make Aristotle's words obsolete if the journey to knowledge is too easy? If AI tools simply give you all the answers, then will there be no struggle, no deep thinking, nothing memorable about the educational experience?

On the other hand…'A teacher who is attempting to teach without inspiring the pupil with a desire to learn is hammering on cold iron.'

These are the words of Horace Mann, an American educational reformer in the 19th century, who played a key role in promoting and establishing public education in the US.

Could AI unlock the inspiration to learn that eludes so many? The rhetoric is quite stunning.

> These are adaptive machines that adapt to individuals. They will listen to the voices of the learners, read their faces and study them in the way gifted teachers study their students. (Seldon, 2017, p. 9)

As a school leader, I envision AI inspiring the next generation by personalising learning and unlocking each student's potential. AI can tailor lessons to individual needs, making education more engaging and effective. It will provide instant feedback, fostering a growth mindset and continuous improvement.

Beyond the classroom, AI will equip students with the skills to navigate a tech-driven world, encouraging innovation and creativity. By automating administrative tasks, AI allows teachers to focus on mentorship and meaningful interactions. Ultimately, AI will not just enhance learning but will prepare our students to become thoughtful, adaptive leaders of tomorrow.

WHAT OF THE ETHICS OF USING AI IN EDUCATION?

The International Baccalaureate (IB) policy on the ethical use of AI emphasises the responsible and informed integration of AI technologies in education. It advocates for using AI to enhance learning while ensuring students' privacy and data security. The policy encourages educators and students to understand AI's capabilities and limitations, promoting critical thinking and ethical considerations.

It stresses transparency in AI applications and the importance of human oversight to prevent bias and misuse. By fostering a balanced approach, the IB aims to harness AI's potential to enrich education while upholding its core values of integrity, fairness and respect for individual rights.

> The IB will not ban the use of AI software. The simplest reason is that it is an ineffective way to deal with innovation. (International Baccalaureate, 2023)

Perhaps the best advice is to see AI as the latest in a long line of innovations that have catapulted learning forward.

From moveable type, to printing, to public education for all, to access to universities, to the advent of the first personal computers, to the invention of the internet and email, and then the smart phone. Educators should find ways of utilising the benefits and mitigating the risks of using AI technologies just as we have done with every other innovation over the years.

> ## ASIDE
>
> HAL, from *2001: A Space Odyssey*, stands for heuristically programmed algorithmic computer. HAL 9000 was meant to be an advanced AI system designed to manage the spacecraft's operations and assist the crew.
>
> Heuristically refers to a method of problem-solving that employs practical approaches or shortcuts to produce solutions that may not be perfect but are sufficient for immediate goals. Heuristic methods rely on experience-based techniques for learning and discovery, often using trial and error, rules of thumb or educated guesses to achieve results quickly and efficiently.
>
> In the context of AI, heuristics allow systems to make decisions and solve problems based on approximations and previous experiences rather than exhaustive calculations. As shown in the film, there are inherent dangers with this!
>
> AI teaching assistants – discuss!

AI promises so much for teachers, learners, parents and, in fact, all of us. A note of caution is that while time-saving merits are clear and most teachers already use some form of AI — although the systems are not yet perfect — is there a danger that a teacher might simply teach by numbers driven by ChatGPT or a similar large language model?

- How is your SLT reducing staff workload by embracing the very best of AI technology?
- What sorts of policy, training and quality assurance do you need to be sure that lessons are really tailored to your children in your unique context?
- How is AI, in your context, revolutionising assessment, data and tracking to ensure learning is nudged early on to ensure pupils' outcomes improve and their wellbeing is safeguarded?

SELF-REGULATION

> Between stimulus and response, there is a space. In that space is our power to choose our response. In our response lies our growth and our freedom.
>
> Viktor E. Frankl

If you speak to many in the education space today, they will tell you that the number one factor that determines how well youngsters will do at school is the extent to which they are able to self-regulate.

- *Self-regulation is the ability to understand and manage your own behaviour and reactions.*
- *Self-regulation helps children and teenagers learn, behave well, get along with others and become independent.*
- *Self-regulation begins to develop rapidly in the toddler and preschooler years. It continues to develop into adulthood.*
- *Ways to develop your child's self-regulation include talking, planning, problem-solving and role-modelling.*

(raisingchildren.net.au, 2025)

FACTORS THAT NEGATIVELY AFFECT SELF-REGULATION

Self-regulation is a key skill for children, helping them to manage their emotions, behaviour and thoughts. However, several factors can interfere with this ability, making it harder for children to stay in control. Understanding these factors can help us support them in developing stronger self-regulation skills.

One major factor is stress. Whether it's academic pressure, family challenges or social dynamics, stress can overwhelm a child's ability to self-regulate. When their brains are in 'fight or flight' mode, it's tough to focus on anything else. Teaching stress management techniques, like deep breathing or mindfulness, can be a game-changer.

Sleep deprivation is another biggie. A tired brain struggles with impulse control and attention. Ensuring that children get enough sleep can dramatically improve their self-regulation abilities. Establishing a calming bedtime routine can work wonders.

Poor nutrition also plays a role. A diet high in sugar and low in nutrients can lead to energy crashes and mood swings, making it harder for kids to manage their emotions and actions. A balanced diet rich in fruit, vegetables and whole grains fuels the brain and body for better self-control.

Lack of physical activity can also impact self-regulation. Exercise is a natural stress reliever and mood booster. When kids don't move enough, they may find it harder to focus and stay calm. Regular physical activity, whether it's sports, dancing or just playing outside, can help keep their self-regulation skills sharp.

Finally, emotional challenges like anxiety or frustration can hinder self-regulation. Children need tools to express and manage their emotions in healthy ways. Teaching emotional literacy and providing a supportive environment can help them navigate their feelings and maintain self-control.

By addressing these factors – stress, sleep, nutrition, physical activity and emotional health – we can empower children to develop strong self-regulation skills, setting them up for success in school and life.

PARENTING

> When you become a parent, you stop being the picture and start being the frame.
>
> Anon.

Of course, young children do not control (or should not control) their bedtime, what and when they eat, screen time and stress in the family home. So, experienced headteachers and their teams will try to reach out to parents – especially in the early years. When children's centres first opened part of their remit was parenting classes.

A typical UK children's centre parenting programme was designed to support parents and caregivers in raising young children, focusing on enhancing parenting skills, building confidence, and promoting child development and self-regulation. Here is what such a programme might include:

1. Parenting workshops

    Positive parenting techniques: Sessions on effective discipline strategies, understanding child behaviour and fostering positive relationships.

    Child development education: Information on developmental milestones, understanding a child's emotional and social needs, and how to support learning at home.

    Parenting confidence: Building self-esteem and confidence in parents, helping them feel more capable in their parenting roles.

2. Health and wellbeing

    Nutrition and healthy eating: Guidance on preparing healthy meals, understanding nutritional needs and promoting healthy eating habits.

    Mental health support: Workshops and resources to help parents manage stress, anxiety and other mental health challenges. Some centres may offer mindfulness or relaxation techniques.

    Physical activity: Encouraging active lifestyles, with activities that parents and children can enjoy together.

3. Practical support

    Sleep management: Advice on establishing routines and managing sleep issues in young children.

    Toilet training: Support and tips for parents on how to approach and manage toilet training.

Budgeting and financial advice: Guidance on managing household finances, understanding benefits and accessing additional support services.

4. Social and emotional support

    Peer support groups: Providing a space for parents to connect, share experiences and support each other.

    Bonding activities: Structured activities designed to strengthen the parent–child bond, like baby massage or play sessions.

    Relationship support: Advice and resources for managing relationships and communication within the family.

5. Access to additional services

    Signposting to local resources: Information on accessing further support, such as childcare, health services and educational opportunities.

    Specialist support: Some programmes may offer targeted support for specific challenges, such as parenting children with additional needs.

Parents who had difficult childhoods and who suffered from a lack of parenting may lack confidence when meeting the needs of their own family.

'Confident parent, confident children' is more than just a phrase – it's a powerful concept that underscores the importance of a parent's self-assurance in raising resilient and self-assured children. When parents feel confident in their abilities, it creates a positive ripple effect, fostering a home environment where children feel secure, valued and capable.

A confident parent sets clear boundaries and expectations while also showing warmth and understanding. This balance gives children the structure they need, along with the emotional support to explore, learn and develop their own confidence. When parents model self-assurance, children learn by example, internalising the message that they too can face challenges and navigate the world with a strong sense of self-worth.

Moreover, confident parenting is not about having all the answers but about trusting your instincts and being open to learning and growing alongside your children. It's about showing your kids that it's okay to make mistakes, ask for help and try again – skills that are crucial for building their own resilience, confidence and self-regulation.

Programmes that focus on 'confident parent, confident children' often emphasise these aspects, offering parents the tools and support they need to feel more capable in their role. Whether it's through workshops, peer support groups or practical advice, these programmes help parents build the confidence that will ultimately help their children thrive.

In essence, when parents believe in their abilities, they pass on that belief to their children, creating a strong foundation for their future success and wellbeing.

Effective parenting programmes aim to create a nurturing and supportive environment where parents can learn, share and grow, ultimately benefiting both them and their children.

ANGER PROBLEMS

Children who lose their temper regularly for what seems trivial reasons in the classroom and in the playground can really test the patience of the teachers and other children.

Anger management problems in children can stem from a variety of underlying causes. At its core, anger is often a response to frustration, fear of rejection or failure, or a sense of helplessness. Children may struggle with managing anger due to factors such as unmet emotional needs, difficulty in expressing feelings or a lack of appropriate coping mechanisms. Environmental factors, such as stress at home, school pressures or witnessing conflict, can also contribute to a child's inability to regulate anger.

Some children might have a lower tolerance for frustration, possibly due to temperament or developmental issues, making it harder for them to process and respond to challenging situations calmly. Additionally, neurological factors, such as attention deficit hyperactivity disorder or behavioural disorders, can impair a child's impulse control, leading to frequent outbursts.

Addressing these issues requires a compassionate and multifaceted approach.

First, it's important to help children understand and label their emotions.

Teaching them emotional literacy can empower them to express their feelings verbally rather than through anger. Techniques like deep breathing, counting to 10 or using a 'calm-down' space can be effective in helping children manage their immediate reactions.

Some children need a safe space to go when they feel overwhelmed – time out on a beanbag with a sand timer for them to see how long they have been sitting may help them to understand that after five minutes of cooling down it is time to go back to class. Arranging these protocols ahead of time and communicating with everyone will ensure success.

It is also crucial to model appropriate behaviour. Children learn a great deal by observing adults, so parents and caregivers should demonstrate calmness and effective communication, even in stressful situations.

Therapeutic approaches, such as cognitive-behavioural therapy, can help children develop strategies to cope with anger triggers. In some cases, family counselling might be beneficial to address broader dynamics that contribute to the child's anger.

Ultimately, understanding the root causes of a child's anger and equipping them with tools to manage it can transform these challenges into opportunities for emotional growth and resilience.

In primary schools, we know that the class teacher's consistency with the school rules and sanctions is key for a child to start to feel secure and know where the boundaries lie in the school. Building meaningful relationships with vulnerable children can improve their self-esteem, and with each micro-success celebrated, progress can happen. But be prepared for bad days and for kindness to be shredded as some test to what extent you really care about them – the answer is always 'I care enough to teach you a better way to behave and a calmer life to lead.'

Leaders' support of the teacher and teaching assistant with enforcing sanctions is also key – and parent meetings will get heated. Supporting the child in school means leaders support the staff and the parents to create the conditions for success for the child, as they learn to self-regulate and not to be so fearful of failure.

Headteachers who walk the corridors – popping into lessons, catching children being good in the moment – report that positive interactions with 'difficult children' can mean that when conflict leads to difficult discussions with parents, you have some currency in the bank to better deal with the issues.

ASIDE
THE TABARD

In one school, a system of community service was brought in for pupils, usually Year 5 and 6 boys, who didn't yet meet the expectations of the school for their behaviour. The idea was that, as they were regularly and in full view of the rest of the school being rude, disrespectful or fighting, part of their sanctions should be a positive and restorative action to help the school.

In this school at lunchtime a few 'midday assistants' organised the children's lunches and made sure tables were wiped, trays were stacked neatly and children put any waste or rubbish in the bins. For a small group, a weekly routine of sporting the midday tabard as part of their school community service became a familiar sight.

The success of this approach depended on the relationships they had with their class teacher, as they made a point of visiting them in the hall to see the children in action and, of course, gently tease them for wearing the correct personal protection equipment. In fact, in one class, if a child was starting to bubble, a skilful Year 6 teacher would raise an eyebrow and say 'tabard' – after which, behaviour miraculously improved!

The serious point about the power of restorative conversations between staff and children, and consistent sanctions and positive praise for good behaviour, is worth making to your teams.

- How effective are we at repairing strained relationships in the classroom?
- What sanctions and rewards send the right signals to our children and parents?
- To what extent does our school support emotional literacy in its culture, values and curriculum?

TEACHING

Carpe diem – seize the day.

Dead Poets Society (1989)

Many teachers were inspired by Robin Williams's portrayal of Mr Keating in *Dead Poets Society* (Weir, 1989). He seemed to encapsulate a teacher who taught about what it meant to be human – he saw into the pupils' hearts and minds, and he was quirky and interesting and not afraid to take educational risks. Mr Keating is emblematic of the teacher we all wanted to be: insightful, caring, daring and ultimately seen as a guide for the next generation of learners.

Why did you become a teacher? What are you most proud of? What changes would you make if you could to the profession?

School leaders constantly revisit what great teaching means. Essentially it is made up of:

Meaningful relationships + great curriculum + high expectations + researched-based pedagogy

WHAT MAKES A GREAT TEACHER? AND HOW CAN I RETAIN THEM?

A truly great teacher is someone with a passion for education. They spend their time in school working, researching, designing lessons, creating videos, ensuring behaviour is well managed and being a radiator of positive energy. Nothing is too much. At once, a professional and a human being – fun, collegiate and effective. Prepared to say, nicely, if they disagree with a certain direction, but equally prepared to trial something rather than saying it won't work.

These are the teachers that all the parents want next year, all the pupils want next year and who other teachers want to learn from. But when you are that good, the temptation to move on and up can be strong.

> Train people well enough so they can leave. Treat them well enough so they don't have to.
>
> Sir Richard Branson

My advice is:

- Careful performance management – include additional CPD and opportunities externally to showcase excellence.
- Develop your best teachers so they constantly feel valued, at the edge of their professional learning and have a hand on the tiller.

THE IMPACT OF GOOD TEACHING

One headteacher received a message through LinkedIn from a pupil they taught 30 years ago. The past student, Andrew, now 40, wrote the following;

> How are you sir?
>
> I doubt very much you would remember me, but you were my year 5 teacher 1995/96.
>
> Well, recently I have been clearing my parents' loft and came across old photos. I posted them online and it sparked our class's memories and we have been exchanging stories of our primary school years, and namely the coolest and best teacher, which is you, Sir, from singing 'Wonderwall' while you played your guitar, to your approachable and engaging style.
>
> I hope you are keeping well, and it would appear you are enjoying a long and incredible career!
>
> Thanks so much for connecting.

I'm sure we can all recall times when we have received thanks and appreciation from students and parents, and it's so important that we stop to fully recognise them and take them in. It is what one head refers to as 'gold coins that we must deposit in our emotional bank account'.

The reason we must make these affirming deposits for ourselves is that all too often we have situations that deplete us of energy and optimism, when we feel that despite our best endeavours pupils, parents, staff, governors, Ofsted or members of our community, virtual or physical, are unhappy, disappointed, angry or unreasonable.

Teaching children is what brought us into the profession in the first place. Few student teachers on a BEd or PGCE dream of writing the perfect governors' report or setting a clever budget – we dreamed of setting children on the path to full and happy lives. We wanted the sort of warm and respectful relationships with our children and their parents that meant success was guaranteed.

I wonder if we ask our children in school what is occurring when teaching is at its best? Where are you? What's the subject? What say do the children have? Is technology allowed? Can everyone access the learning? Has there been pre-teaching?

I wonder if they might say, when teaching is at its best, 'Our teacher is happy, enthusiastic, funny, firm but fair, knows their stuff and can explain so we get it.'

THE PROMISE AND THE REALITY

Teacher training colleges in the UK paint an enticing picture of the profession, and with good reason. Their glossy brochures and enthusiastic recruiters promise a career filled with purpose, creativity and the profound satisfaction of shaping young lives. They highlight the joy of inspiring students, the camaraderie of the staffroom and the promise of long holidays (a phrase that makes any experienced teacher chuckle).

The message is clear: teaching is a noble calling, a career that matters, and one that offers job security, progression and personal fulfilment.

And the reality? Well, it's both exactly as promised and vastly different. The sense of purpose is real – there's nothing quite like seeing a student thrive because of your support. Creativity does play a role, but it can be squeezed by curriculum demands and ever-growing administrative tasks. The workload is heavier than most recruits anticipate, and those 'long holidays' are often punctuated by planning, marking and training.

However, the camaraderie is no myth. Teachers form deep bonds through shared challenges and victories. And while the early years can be tough, many find that once they hit their stride, teaching is exactly what was promised: a demanding but deeply rewarding vocation.

The challenge for those that employ teachers is to protect them from the ebb and flow of political whim. To ensure that initial teacher training and their early career is based on educational research and proven best practices. To ensure that experienced mentors can encourage and support the growth of the next generation of teachers, so they can become the teacher that will make the difference in young people's lives.

Further training and a good salary is key to keeping the best teachers in our schools – too many Mr/Ms Keatings leave disillusioned and frustrated to take on better paid but ultimately less satisfying employment.

Reflect

- What effective recruitment and retention schemes run in your school or trust?
- Can you be proactive in spotting talented teachers that start to wobble and put in support before they leave?
- What role do teaching unions and professional associations have to lobby the government to improve the system?
- How do governing bodies play a part in retention?

WHAT WE TEACH

> It ain't what you do it's the way that you do it, and that's what gets results!
>
> Melvin 'Sy' Oliver and James 'Trummy' Young

So, how important is the 'what' of education? We are in an endless debate about skills or content as teachers, concerned with the scope and sequence of planning documents. When you stop and think about it, in this digital age, why do we teach children handwriting, spelling and grammar? Surely, if we gave every child a device, they could dictate what they want to say directly into a document that could then be spell-checked and massaged by grammar software. We already do this for students with additional needs – so why not for all?

Are we stuck with an enlightenment model of education based on religious teaching? A congregation sit and listen, and the pastor reads the lesson for them to remember and copy out?

Indeed, with AI, a well-crafted prompt could deliver what appears to be a well-rounded and informed response from a few key words. The value of precise language use and oracy just increased!

While it's true that the digital age of the 1980s and 1990s is now being superseded by the age of technological augmentation, it's also true to state that these AI resources do not trump HI – human intelligence. At the time of writing, large language models are wonderful research aids, scaffolds and time savers. They are not (yet) Shakespeare, Brontë or Gibran.

We teach children to understand the world around them, the people in it and, above all else, themselves. We could achieve this by teaching astronomy, anthropology and psychology. Our curriculum choices in the West tend to be based on a classical view of a hierarchy of subjects.

***

Digression

When I was finishing my BEd – a primary course majoring in science – we concluded with a leadership module. During this module, we had to prioritise the curriculum and present how we might lead a model school. In every case we started with an apology to the expressive arts. Talented and enthusiastic art, drama, PE and music teachers were sidelined. Despite four years of honing their skills and creating art galleries, musical concerts, sport and dance events, and dramatic productions, the core subjects dominated. And we took this view with us into schools.

***

Many people looking back on their school days will say they don't remember much of what they were taught – for example, algebra and trigonometry derided as a complete waste of time as most see no practical application. However, you could also argue that most of the population will not become artists, musicians, actors or sports stars, but we still benefit from these educational experiences, leaving many with a love of poetry, music appreciation or a more active lifestyle.

But learning to learn in an increasingly changing world – that's future proofing learning. In other words, we stop delivering topics for their own sake – and, instead, the topic is a vehicle to learn 'how I learn best'.

Many thought leaders in education will lean on research that demonstrates clear correlations between a structured approach to language acquisition and greater than expected progress. This focus on vocabulary, with its chant of 'if you can say it, you can write it', is entrenched with a distinct approach. Some of the research points to the following areas as key to increased pupil progress:

- Reducing cognitive load.
- Retrieval practice.
- Interleaving.
- Clear and consistent learning practices and routines.

The work of Professor John Hattie (2008) on effect size shows that it is the quality of the teacher and the quality of their feedback to students that can have a high positive impact.

Alongside this is the notion of teaching children the skills of learning and remembering. The classrooms where metacognition is woven into the language of learning are those with the best chance of closing learning gaps and accelerating progress for all.

So, does it matter what we teach?

Yes and no. A student may get a rounded education with history, geography, maths, science and English as well as art, PE and drama. Arguably, this may be a surface-level education and, over time, the relevance and recall of it will fade.

But teach a child to think critically, how to ask the right questions, how to research, how to communicate in English and another language – now you're talking about a toolkit that will support the mythical life-long learner.

In essence, this is not an either/or but and an and/and.

What schools are seeing in their data when they use educational research to shape their teaching is great strides in progress. Why? Because teaching less but in more depth, with a focus on vocabulary, with reduced cognitive load during the explanation phase and challenging all to think hard and deeply is paying off. Returning again and again to key concepts ensures that most children are moving the experience into their long-term memories, enabling them to recall and use the learning months later.

One powerful example is Curriculum Unity Schools Partnership (CUSP) – see the 'Aside' below.

***

This has been an extended chapter about teaching and learning; it has been the very bread and butter of schools since ancient times. We know that high quality teaching matters and that selecting the right teaching styles at the right time brings out the best in our primary children.

Schools today look equally carefully at what they teach, the schemes of work, the curriculum intent, implementation and impact. Leaders have their own preferences and shape those with their teams. These are personal decisions within professional frameworks, always with an eye on what is working for the children we serve in each setting.

> ## ASIDE
>
> CUSP was written by Alex Bedford and Lauren Meadows (see https://www.unity-curriculum.co.uk/more-information/primary). What it does effectively is to show teachers how they put educational research to use in their classrooms. This is not a new approach. There are others — for example, John Hattie's Visible Learning or High Performance Learning.
>
> The CUSP approach is guided by evidence-led curriculum structures, such as retrieval, spaced retrieval practice and interleaving. It is underpinned by explicit vocabulary instruction and research-focused pedagogy.
>
> Combining these has led to exceptional outcomes for pupils, as a result of coherent curriculum design and instructional teaching. It also gives school leaders consistency and expectations. CUSP is unapologetically ambitious — it does not only improve outcomes for pupils but also teacher subject knowledge.
>
> ### TEACHING CUSP AT A LESSON LEVEL
>
> A CUSP lesson typically follows a structured approach that is divided into distinct phases, each designed to support effective teaching and deep learning (see Figure 3). The phases of a CUSP lesson are:
>
> | Connect | Explain | Example | Attempt | Apply | Challenge |
> |---|---|---|---|---|---|
> | Activate prior learning | Instruct vocabulary Explain core concepts | High-quality modelling Explicit direct instruction (My turn) | Guided practice Gradually reduce scaffold (Our turn) | Independent practice Application of new concept (Your turn) | Deepen understanding Sophisticate thinking Structured reflection |
>
> *Figure 3. The six elements of a CUSP lesson*
>
> *Source:* Unity Schools Partnership

UNDERSTANDING

If you want understanding, try giving some.

Malcom Forbes

If I were to summarize in one sentence the single most important principle I have learned in the field of interpersonal relations, it would be this: seek first to understand, then to be understood.

Stephen R. Covey

In school leadership, 'Seek first to understand, then to be understood' should be your mantra. It's like being the Sherlock Holmes of education – you can't solve the case (or lead effectively) without first gathering all the clues. The best leaders don't bulldoze their way into a room with answers; they walk in with questions, ready to listen.

Here's the thing: when you focus on understanding first, you unlock a treasure trove of insights. You learn what's really driving that teacher's frustration or why a parent is concerned. This doesn't just make you more informed – it makes you more relatable. People feel heard, valued and respected when you take the time to understand their perspective. That's leadership gold.

But it's not just about making others feel warm and fuzzy. When you truly understand the issues, you can craft solutions that hit the mark. No more generic fixes – your responses are targeted, thoughtful and effective. This earns you credibility, making it much easier to get buy-in when it's your turn to be understood.

Further, seeking to understand first is a power move for building trust. Staff and students are more likely to follow someone who gets them. They'll open up, share ideas and work harder because they know you're in their corner. And when you do share your own views, they're more likely to listen, because they know you've already taken the time to listen to them.

So, instead of charging in with your agenda, pause. Listen. Understand. It might take a little more time, but the pay-off is huge: stronger relationships, better decisions and a school culture where everyone feels they're part of something meaningful. In short, it's not just better to seek first to understand – it's essential for truly effective school leadership.

WHAT DO THE CHILDREN ACTUALLY UNDERSTAND?

As teachers we spend most of our time in lessons, planning for lessons or assessing the learning that happened in lessons. We build up a picture of each child over time from our shared teacher/pupil experience of 'how we teach' and 'how they receive and practise' the knowledge, skills and understanding we deliver. Some of that is daily questions and answers and work in books, while other conclusions may be drawn from progress over time.

But what of pupil data? There's a lot of it about – which data do you use? How are you selective in a spirit of 'less is more'?

- Baselines
- Benchmarks
- CATS
- SATs
- GL
- New Group Reading Test
- Phonics screening
- Summative and formative
- Project-based
- Moderation
- Matrix

- Rubric
- Skills
- Knowledge
- Understanding
- Pupil Attitudes to Self and School survey
- Wellbeing
- Fischer Family Trust

Reflect
- What have I missed from your school's assessment calendar?
- Do you over-test your pupils?
- How else can you gather performance data without testing?
- How effectively is pupil data used at individual, class, cohort and school level?
- Could data be relied upon to show us what needs to improve to secure a decent education for this young person, so they can be financially independent?
- Could you set a challenging target of 90% of pupils meeting expectations, or better, in your school?

THE NEUROSCIENCE OF UNDERSTANDING

Learning rewires your brain. Imagine your neurons, those tiny brain cells, are links in a chain. When you learn something new, you're essentially teaching these neurons how to connect. At first the connections are weak and fade easily, but with practice they become stronger, forming intricate, graceful patterns. This is called neuroplasticity – the brain's ability to change its structure and function based on experience.

HOW DO I GET CHILDREN TO REMEMBER?

Many teachers recall teaching a lesson on, for example, using a comma, then a few days later trying to apply this knowledge and discovering that the children have 'forgotten' what you taught them. One explanation is that something taught in isolation without context sits in the short-term memory for a day or two, then dissolves from memory. If I ask you to recall your earliest memory, the chances are there was an emotional response attached to it at the time – for example, being locked under the stairs by your older brother.

Should we seek to bring emotion into aspects of our teaching, then, to make certain key facts memorable? Poetry, art, history and English literature lend themselves to this. But can you make physics emotional? I'm sure that with the right preamble, teaching about the Earth in Space, the cosmos and our part in it could bring a bit of awe and wonder.

Memory is like your brain's filing system, except that it's more like a highly creative librarian who sometimes misplaces things. When you learn something new, your brain first stores it in short-term memory – think of it as a sticky note on your mental fridge. But sticky notes fall off, so to keep that knowledge around, your brain needs to transfer it to long-term memory. This happens through a process called consolidation, often occurring during sleep.

For teachers, the goal is to help students move information from those sticky notes into the more permanent files. One powerful method is spaced repetition – revisiting material over time, not cramming it all at once. This method works because it strengthens the neural pathways, making it easier for students to recall information later.

Another tip is to make learning multisensory. The more senses involved, the more neural connections are formed. For example, pairing visuals with text or incorporating movement into lessons can help cement ideas. This turns learning into an engaging experience, not just a memorisation task.

Storytelling is also a fantastic tool. Our brains are wired to remember stories better than isolated facts, so framing lessons as narratives can make the material more relatable and memorable.

Lastly, encourage active recall. Instead of just re-reading notes, have students quiz themselves or teach the material to a peer. This active engagement forces the brain to retrieve information, strengthening memory.

UNDERSTANDING

In short, making learning interactive, spaced out and narrative-driven helps students to file away what they've learned in the brain's long-term storage where it's easier to find later.

Hermann Ebbinghaus (1850-1909) was a pioneering German psychologist who conducted groundbreaking experiments on memory. Through his research, he discovered that information retention decreases exponentially over time if there is no active review or reinforcement.

The Ebbinghaus 'forgetting curve' illustrates how quickly memory deteriorates, showing a significant decline in recall within the first 24 hours after learning, unless strategies like repetition are employed. Ebbinghaus's work laid the foundation for modern cognitive psychology and has greatly influenced educational strategies, particularly in areas such as spaced repetition and memory enhancement techniques.

ACTIVE LEARNING

Active learning isn't just a catchy slogan – it is clearly backed by brain science. When kids 'do', they move beyond passive absorption to active engagement, turning knowledge into experience. Research shows that hands-on activities, like experiments or role-playing, fire up multiple brain regions, making connections stronger and learning deeper.

This multisensory approach helps kids not just see or hear information but truly understand it by applying, analysing and creating. It's like upgrading from watching a cooking show to actually whipping up the dish yourself – because when kids get their hands dirty, the learning sticks and understanding flourishes.

Ten top tips for creating active learning experiences in the primary classroom

1. Incorporate hands-on activities – Use manipulatives, experiments or craft projects to make abstract concepts tangible. This helps students grasp ideas by directly engaging with materials.
2. Use think-pair-share – Encourage students to think about a question individually, discuss it with a partner, and then share with the class. This promotes collaboration and deeper understanding.

3. Integrate technology – Utilise interactive tools like educational apps, online quizzes or virtual field trips to make learning dynamic and engaging.
4. Implement role-playing – Have students act out historical events, literary characters or science concepts. This immersive approach makes learning memorable.
5. Create learning stations – Set up different activity stations around the room, each focusing on a specific skill or concept. Students rotate, keeping them active and engaged.
6. Encourage project-based learning – Let students work on projects that require problem-solving, creativity and the application of knowledge, fostering a deeper connection with the material.
7. Incorporate movement – Use activities like 'walk and talk' discussions or kinaesthetic games that combine learning with physical movement to boost engagement and memory.
8. Use real-world examples – Connect lessons to students' lives with examples from their environment or current events, making learning relevant and meaningful.
9. Facilitate peer teaching – Let students teach each other. Explaining concepts to peers solidifies their own understanding and builds communication skills.
10. Ask open-ended questions – Encourage critical thinking by asking questions that require more than a yes or no answer, prompting students to explore and express their ideas.

> ## ASIDE
> ### USE IT OR LOSE IT
> Research on London taxi drivers, conducted by Dr Eleanor Maguire and her team, revealed remarkable changes in the brain, specifically in the hippocampus, a region associated with spatial navigation and memory (Maguire et al., 2000).
>
> The study, part of the famous 'Knowledge' training research, showed that taxi drivers developed an enlarged posterior hippocampus due to their extensive mental mapping of London streets. However, after retirement, this hippocampal enlargement diminished, reflecting reduced use of spatial navigation skills. This finding highlighted the brain's neuroplasticity – its ability to adapt and change with experience – and underscored how active engagement in complex tasks shapes, and is shaped by, neural structures over time.
>
> - What techniques for learning have you found that really deepen children's understanding?
> - What topics and subject matter extend, say, Year 2s or Year 5s – the same or different?
> - Set Hermann Ebbinghaus and Dr Eleanor Maguire as a comparative research topic for Year 5 and Year 6 classes – they'll love it!

VISION

Vision is seeing the masterpiece while you are mixing the paints.

Robert Henri

This quote is attributed to Robert Henri, an American painter and teacher, who was a leading figure of the Ashcan School of American realism. He believed in the importance of an artist's vision and the ability to see the potential and final outcome of a work, even while in the process of creation. Henri's teachings and writings have influenced many artists and are often quoted in discussions about creativity and artistic process.

As a school leader who knows where the organisation is heading, what the destination could look like and taking people with you are so important. This idea of 'followership' is the art of influencing, convincing and inspiring people that life would be better over here – and when we get to the other side of this mountain, we will have all succeeded.

But whose vision is it, anyway?

One primary head tells the tale of turning up at his second headship – with a vision statement from the previous school on a USB drive to lead an INSET day on 'Our New Vision'. You can guess what happened – 'this is not our school or our vision'. Impatient to get moving on improving the school, this young headteacher missed the crucial step of building a consensus.

It seems obvious but…

A shared vision that has been constructed by the community is much more likely to stick. When stakeholders have had time to discuss and debate the problems, the gaps, the successes and the shared hopes for the future – this is when a collective vision is most likely to turn into constructive collective action.

EXPECTATIONS

Many heads face a story that starts: 'Kids around here are so low academically when they join that we have no way of meeting age-related attainment – you know what the estate is like. Parents don't come in unless they are angry, staff don't stay long – it's a miracle we do as well as we do.'

Any journey of improvement that is going to work and improve life chances for young people starts in the polar opposite way: 'I will tell you what we can expect from these children – every bit as much as children from more privileged areas. These children are tough, resilient, and want to have jobs and lead happy and interesting lives. Let's demand the best from them in terms of attendance, behaviour and work ethic and watch them rise to those expectations!'

Challenging the status quo is tricky. You want to shift rather casual talk about 'aspiration' and embed 'expectation' as the dominant vocabulary. Your team will need to quickly agree the key priorities and be consistent day after day. Consistency says, 'We mean what we say, nicely, but also we care about you (pupils), and you can do better.' A few quick wins will show the doubters inside and outside the school that things are improving, and slowly the tide will start to change in the children's favour.

'But we did that five years ago and it didn't work…'

You have heard this one – it's the 'blockers' go-to excuse for positive change. The advice here is to explain why it will be different this time with proper training, resources and support.

There is power in a pilot or proof of concept. Where people are reluctant to try a new approach, the idea of a trial to see if it actually works can be helpful. This reduces the stakes from 'We are all doing this forever' to 'Let's try it and see'.

One example of this was when one headteacher wanted to start a children's centre. Initially, sceptical staff and reluctant parents didn't see how this fitted into a school setting. However, when the community saw the impact that occurs when you pour some children's centre goodness into an early years setting, they realised that this was exactly the action required to bring the school vision of a vibrant learning community to life.

WALKING THE WALK – VISION INTO PRACTICE

Walking the walk of school improvement requires more than just plans and aspirations though – it demands action, commitment and a shared vision that inspires every member of the school community. Most school principals believe that genuine improvement starts with listening deeply to your teachers, students and families. We must celebrate what's working while being fearless in identifying areas for growth.

Improvement is not a one-time initiative but a continuous journey where every step, no matter how small, brings us closer to excellence.

In this process, data becomes our guide, helping us to make informed decisions. But it's the human element – our passion, collaboration and resilience – that truly drives change. We must create a culture where innovation thrives, where educators feel empowered to try new approaches and where mistakes are seen as learning opportunities. No-blame culture.

Our focus is on developing a rich, supportive environment where every student can excel. This means prioritising professional development for teachers, fostering a positive school climate and engaging families as partners in education. By consistently modelling these values and maintaining high expectations, we build momentum. Together, we are not just talking about improvement; we are living it, day by day, transforming our school into a place of possibility and success for all.

KEY PERFORMANCE INDICATORS

So, what does success look like? The traditional school improvement plan will have pages of actions and success criteria. Some headteachers find that a short summary of key priorities with some key performance indicators helps to keep teams focused on the most important things first. We must be aware of 'mission creep' as the weeks go by and events start to overtake a school. Keep to the plan and remember to allow time for monitoring, evaluation and review.

If you were to ask your receptionist, teaching assistants, caretaker or children, would they know what the school is working on to improve this year? How might your team remedy this?

Success criteria – be SMART

SMART is a tried and tested acronym and probably presented on almost every leadership course. It really is one that is worth thinking about afresh, as often as you can stand.

Defining clearly what success looks like before you start makes it easier for staff to work towards this and, of course, to know when you have collectively achieved this.

SMART targets are a dynamic tool for setting clear, achievable goals that propel our school community forward. SMART stands for specific, measurable, achievable, relevant, and time-bound – each element ensuring that our objectives are not just dreams but actionable steps towards success.

- Specific targets mean clarity. We're not just saying 'improve reading scores' but rather 'increase Grade 3 reading comprehension by 10% within six months'. This sharp focus helps everyone know exactly what we're aiming for.
- Measurable ensures we can track progress. By defining what success looks like – whether through test scores, attendance rates or behavioural metrics – we can celebrate victories along the way and adjust our strategies if needed.
- Achievable reminds us to be ambitious yet realistic. Goals should stretch us but remain within reach, keeping motivation high and preventing burnout.
- Relevant connects each target to our broader mission. Every goal must align with our school's vision, ensuring that every effort contributes to meaningful improvement.

- Time-bound adds urgency. Deadlines motivate action and keep us accountable, transforming long-term aspirations into short-term wins.

To make the most of SMART targets, involve your team in setting them, regularly review progress and be ready to pivot if circumstances change. By using SMART targets, we turn our school improvement plan into a focused, energising roadmap for success!

ASIDE

When you are trying to communicate your school vision it helps to have three things. This example is from a school in the UAE.

1. A short vision statement.
2. A visual representation of your vision – as a picture speaks a thousand words (see Figure 4).
3. A school motto like 'achieving together'.

There will then be clear strategic intentions for all to see.

We are basing everything we do on what we value. These values will lead to the desired character traits, and these will enable our learner profiles to flower and bloom over the coming years.

If you can manage to locate this in your local context, so much the better.

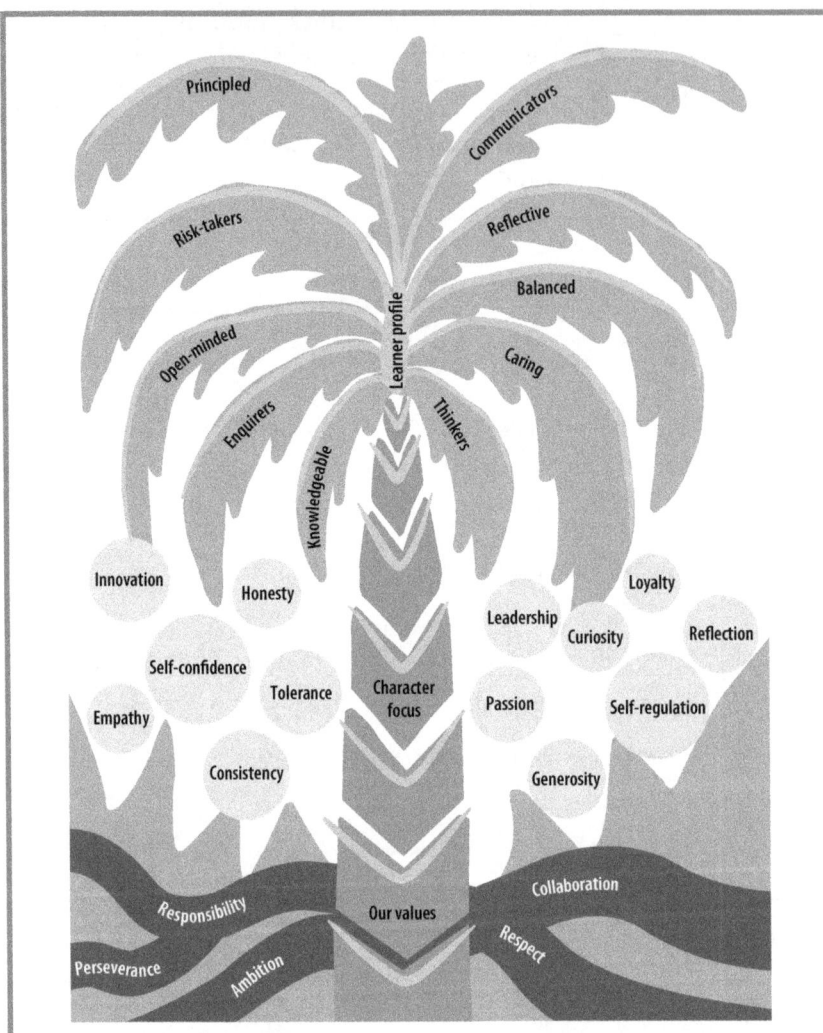

Figure 4. How values lead to character traits, which lead to a learner profile

Source: Khalifa Bin Zayed Al Awal School

WAYNE

They give me diagnostic tests,
they try out reading schemes,
but none of them will ever know
the colour of my dreams.

Peter Dixon

In my second year of primary teaching, I had a mixed Year 5/6 class. As I scanned the class list my eyes landed on Wayne. I knew him from our playground interactions where he would regularly come and stand close to me on the windy days as autumn turned to winter. He had learning difficulties, and his speech was a bit unclear.

I could tell by how he presented that things must be challenging for him. He had close-cropped hair and big blue eyes. One day, Wayne came to complain to me that 'The boys are being mean to me.' Then he leaned in conspiratorially and said quietly, 'They called me the 'F' word.' I replied that I was sorry this had happened and that I would talk to the boys. Then I asked him to tell me the word they had used.

'Fik,' said Wayne indignantly. From that moment on, Wayne and I enjoyed a friendly relationship where I would gently tease him, encourage him and try to build his self-confidence. For example, our class had the topic of 'Ancient Greeks'. 'What's a Greek urn?' 'About £19 a week!' (That joke was first used by Aristotle in 321 BCE.)

***

Increasing self-esteem in students with SEND is transformative – it's like igniting a spark that lights up their entire educational journey. When students with SEND believe in themselves, their world expands. Suddenly, challenges become opportunities, and limitations turn into possibilities.

Imagine a student who once felt overshadowed by their peers, who now steps confidently into the classroom, eager to participate, to try, to learn. This shift isn't just about feeling good; it's about unlocking potential. Self-esteem empowers these students to take risks, embrace new challenges and push beyond the boundaries of what they thought possible.

But the impact doesn't stop with academic subjects. With increased self-esteem, students with SEND begin to flourish socially, building friendships and participating more fully in the life of the school. Their sense of belonging deepens, and they start to see themselves as valued members of the community. This gives them a strong sense of personal and collective identity.

This ripple effect reaches families, who witness their children's growth with pride, and often some relief, and it transforms classrooms into more inclusive, empathetic spaces. Teachers also benefit, as they see their efforts leading to real, meaningful change. Ultimately, boosting self-esteem in students with SEND not only changes their lives – it enriches the entire school environment, creating a culture of possibility and success for everyone.

The power of extracurricular activities can be profound for children as they start to feel success in the art club, the netball team, the eco club, the school production and the steam team!

Building a culture that skyrockets children's self-esteem and motivation is like crafting the perfect recipe – one part encouragement, two parts challenge, with a generous dash of fun. Picture a school where every hallway hums with the energy of discovery, where students feel safe to stumble because they know it's all part of the dance of learning.

ADVICE

Start with a celebration culture – where even the smallest victories are treated like winning the World Cup. Did Jimmy finally crack that maths problem? Cue the applause! Recognition fuels confidence, and confident children are unstoppable.

Next, mix in collaborative projects that make pupils feel like superheroes on a mission. When students work together to solve real-world problems, they don't just learn – they own their achievements. Plus, who doesn't love the camaraderie of a team? (Teamwork makes the dream work, after all!)

Don't forget creative outlets. Art, music, drama – they're all VIP tickets to self-expression. When children see their ideas come to life, their sense of self-worth blossoms.

Top it off with a growth mindset attitude, where mistakes are just pit stops on the road to success. When children learn that perseverance is cooler than perfection, motivation skyrockets.

In a nutshell, create a culture of celebration, collaboration, creativity and resilience, and watch as students' self-esteem and motivation soar to new heights.

Wayne's world

Wayne was a hands-on learner and liked to do rather than listen, and writing was a particular challenge.

I well remember asking my head of inclusion for help with meeting Wayne's needs in the classroom. At the same time, other parents wanted their children to be ready for the dreaded 11+ grammar school entrance exam. Lynne's face lit up, and with infectious enthusiasm she said we could open 'Wayne's Greek market stall'. So it was that over the weeks that followed, Wayne and our class teaching assistant, supported by the head of inclusion, constructed a market stall.

It was basically a few tables with a backdrop printed by Wayne with Greek-style block printing. We added to the environment with fabrics, artwork, pottery, drawings, fact files, topic books and a stall where Wayne sold his goods – plastic goods mainly. I'm not sure if technically the Ancient Greeks had croissants, but Wayne beamed as he sold his goods to his classmates who entered into this imaginary world with him – and accepted him.

I remember one child asking for a discount. Wayne scowled – 'No way, it's five coins, not three' – and the children following this imaginary world's rules, where Wayne was talented with bargaining, allowed him to succeed – and for an hour or two a day 'Wayne's world' was the best place to be. As a new teacher, I learned more from that little boy than he ever learned from me about perseverance, humour and facing your reality.

Nurture groups

Many students are coming to school from tricky backgrounds and home lives. Again, it's worth underlining that school is often an island of certainty in some pupils' chaotic lives.

There is huge value in wraparound care if the budgets will stretch. Breakfast clubs bring a calm and consistent start to the day for many children (and some staff), and after-school care can support working parents as well as students.

For some children, though, a more intense programme of support is needed. Many heads report the success of nurture groups. You will all know or have known pupils with aggressive behaviour, outbursts of anger, poor social skills and very often zero self-esteem.

Nurture groups in primary schools are a powerful intervention rooted in the belief that every child can thrive with the right emotional and social support. Based on attachment theory, these small, structured groups provide a safe, predictable environment where children can build trust, confidence and positive relationships.

The theory behind nurture groups is simple yet profound. Children who have experienced early trauma or disruption may struggle with the social and emotional demands of a typical classroom. Nurture groups address this by replicating the secure, nurturing environment that may have been missing in their early years. They focus on developing self-esteem, resilience and the essential social skills needed for learning and interacting with others.

The power of nurture groups lies in their ability to transform lives. By working in a smaller, more personalised setting, children receive the targeted support they need to address emotional barriers and re-engage with learning. These groups help students understand and manage their emotions, develop a sense of belonging and gain the confidence to participate fully in school life.

Over time, the benefits blossom, not only improving academic outcomes but also creating a more inclusive and empathetic school environment. Nurture groups show that with care and understanding, every child can reach their full potential.

The barriers to nurture groups are often financial, but having the physical space to set up a classroom based on the home environment can also be challenging.

A useful link is: https://www.nurtureuk.org/supporting-you/nurture-groups.

ASIDE

Read Peter Dixon's poem 'The Colour of My Dreams' about dyslexia at https://www.dyslexia-assist.org.uk/_webedit/uploaded-files/All%20Files/Colour%20of%20My%20Dreams.pdf.

REFLECT

- How is the school day for your youngsters with additional needs? Why not spend half a day tracking their experience of inclusion – are they really included or just sitting in the same room?

XENIAL

A well-known Arabic proverb on hospitality is:

الضيف يأتي برزقه (The guest brings his own provision.)

This reflects the belief that a guest is a blessing, and their arrival brings good fortune. It underscores the importance of hospitality in Arabic culture, where welcoming a guest is seen as both a duty and a privilege.

CULTIVATING A CULTURE OF WARMTH AND HOSPITALITY

As a pillar of your educational community, your role extends beyond administration; you shape the very heart of your school culture. Let's delve into the vibrant concept of 'xenial', which captures the essence of hospitality and warmth in relationships.

'Xenial', derived from the Greek word xenia, embodies the spirit of generous hospitality and the positive interactions between host and guest. In the context of our schools, being xenial means fostering an environment where everyone – students, teachers, parents and visitors – feels genuinely welcomed and valued.

Imagine walking through your school doors and being greeted with a smile, a sense of belonging, and a welcoming atmosphere that encourages open communication and collaboration. This is the power of a xenial approach. It creates a supportive and inclusive community where diverse perspectives are celebrated and every individual feels they are a vital part of the school's fabric.

Many headteachers will say they can tell what type of school they are about to visit by the quality of the school's reception area, the warmth of the receptionist and to what extent the children are represented in displays. A school culture starts as you walk up the drive and into the building.

By embracing xenial principles, you set the stage for a thriving educational environment. It enhances relationships, boosts morale, and inspires a culture of kindness and respect. As leaders, your commitment to hospitality can transform our schools into beacons of positivity and excellence.

Let's champion xenial values, making our schools places where everyone feels at home and empowered to achieve their best. Together, we can cultivate an educational landscape that radiates warmth and fosters lifelong connections!

BELONGING

We all want to feel that we belong in our family home, in our school, in our work and in our town and country. When we link pupil attendance to school culture we often see that in schools where communities feel that this is our school, where we belong, attendance, behaviour and achievement improve.

So, what are the ingredients to belonging to a school? Part of the story is the quality and depth of relationships. In schools where they talk about 'achieving together', relationships bring the learning community closer together in the common pursuit of improvement. How can teachers achieve together, pupils and pupils achieve together, and, of course, teachers and pupils and parents and teachers achieve together (see Figure 5)?

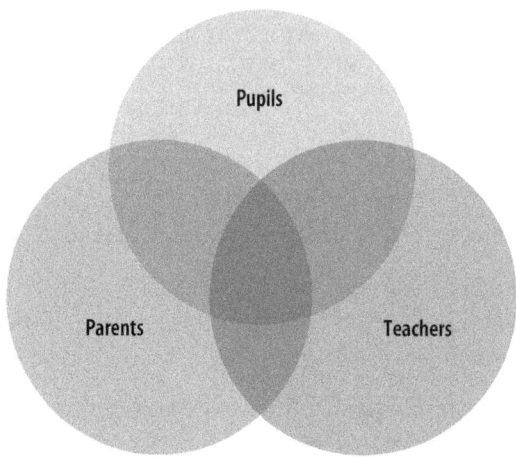

Figure 5. The powerful home-school partnership

In the intersections of these relationships lies the truth about how a pupil's motivation, inspiration, and collaboration with their parents and teachers gives rise to a sense of momentum for a child, cohort and school. In the very centre is the individual child, and their future will depend to a large extent on how attached they feel to the school they attend, how comfortable they feel, and how they see themselves in the staff, curriculum and ambitions laid out and modelled by the ecosystem.

A review on belonging, led by Professor Kathryn Riley with Dr Tracey Allen and Dr Max Coates and published by the National Education Union (NEU), examined the current literature and school case studies. They found that a focus on place and belonging in both policy and practice supports positive learning and a range of good outcomes.

> *Belonging is the sense of being somewhere you can be confident that you will fit in and feel safe in who you are. However, the number of young people who feel they do not belong in school continues to rise, as do rates of exclusion. (UCL Institute of Education, 2020)*

A commitment to develop belonging has led to reductions in student absenteeism, increased staff wellbeing and motivation, and other positive social outcomes including health and wellbeing. Kathryn Riley, professor of urban education at the Institute of Education, said:

> *For many children and young people today home and community are not fixed, and schools represent one of the few points of continuity and stability in their lives. Covid-19 has sent a shockwave across the Globe, exposed the divisions within and across society and thrown a spotlight on the lives of children and young people. It has also reinforced the importance of schools as places of belonging. (UCL Institute of Education, 2020)*

Where children feel they don't belong and are not wanted, the research shows increased rates of exclusion and negative impact on young people's wellbeing.

Dr Riley says in schools that cultivate belonging, there is an emphasis on relationships. The aim of the school is to create a sense of place, belonging and agency: 'We found that intentional whole-school practice can help create a climate of welcome and belonging in school for all.'

Reflect

- How can your school devote quality time so staff can develop whole-school strategies for their context and community so all feel they belong?
- What does intentional whole-school practice mean in a school?

ASIDE

CHRIS OF ARABIA

At the heart of Arabic culture lies hospitality – not just a practice, but a deep-rooted value that defines social interactions. In Arabic society, the guest is treated like royalty, whether they're a friend or a stranger. Welcoming someone into your home is seen as an honour, and generosity flows without hesitation. Traditional customs, like offering coffee or dates, aren't just gestures, they're symbols of respect and warmth.

A guest's comfort is paramount, and often considered a reflection of the host's character. Hospitality is woven into daily life and religious teachings, creating a culture where sharing food, stories and laughter builds connections. Even in the modern era, this hospitality remains strong, from homes to bustling souks.

In Arabic culture, the guest isn't just visiting – they're embraced as part of the family, reinforcing bonds and leaving a lasting impression of genuine care and respect.

Arabic hospitality extends far beyond the home. Whether in the desert, where the Bedouins honour ancient traditions of offering shelter and food, or in cities, where inviting someone for a meal is the ultimate show of goodwill, the spirit is the same. There's a saying: 'The guest is a gift from God,' which perfectly encapsulates the respect and importance of visitors in Arabic society.

NEXT STEP

Start a learning walk from outside your school into the reception area. What do you notice? From cleanliness and the flower beds, to signage (what languages should be represented?) and the welcome from the receptionist, what does your school's first impressions say about how welcoming your school is to the community? First impressions last as we know.

Could you tell where in the world you are, what you value and celebrate, and who your team is from your displays, artwork and photographs? To what extent does this reflect the community you serve, and is the ambition for your children shining out like a lighthouse from the very first interaction with parents and visitors?

YOURSELF

Always be a first-rate version of yourself and not a second rate version of someone else.

Judy Garland

The headteacher role is a multifaceted, complicated, difficult and deeply satisfying role. How do new headteachers begin to play this role?

- 'I'll just observe how the school runs for a term…'
- 'I'll drive a Hummer through this organisation!'
- 'It's all about a shared vision – lets have lots of workshops!'
- 'Here's my vision – it worked in my last school – on we go!'
- 'In my last school we…'

Some heads have one-to-one meetings with all staff to hear directly what their perceptions are about the school's current strengths and areas for development. Others love a SWOT analysis – charting out with staff, pupils, parents and governors what the school's strengths, weaknesses, opportunities and threats are. What are the immediate priorities? (Shoot the crocodile nearest the boat!). Do you go for teaching and learning, curriculum, attitudes to learning, attendance, assessment, middle leaders or parent partnership?

All this activity – when added to the school's academic performance – gives the primary headteacher the what we are going to do.

The how depends on you and how you use your leadership teams.

The advice here from many is 'be yourself'! It can be tempting to impersonate your favourite headteacher or senior leaders from your dim and distant past. The cast list includes the following:

1. The cheerleader: Always positive and energetic, this principal boosts morale with endless enthusiasm and pep talks.
2. Down with the kids: Laid-back and effortlessly charming, they know every student's name and always seem to have the perfect advice. (Beware of becoming 'David Brent'!)
3. The drill sergeant: Disciplined and structured, this principal runs a tight ship and believes in strict rules and high standards.
4. The tech guru: Enthusiastic about all things digital, they introduce cutting-edge technology to the school and encourage tech-savvy teaching.
5. The counsellor: Empathetic and nurturing, this principal always has an open door and a kind word, offering support and guidance to everyone.
6. The visionary: Full of big ideas and ambitious plans, they are constantly thinking of new ways to improve the school and inspire greatness.
7. The old-school traditionalist: Prefers chalkboards (and possibly throwing board rubbers) to smartboards and believes in tried-and-true methods, often reminiscing about 'the good old days'.
8. The sports fanatic: Passionate about physical education and school sports teams, this principal is often seen at games encouraging the school spirit.
9. The bookworm: Always carrying a stack of books, this principal loves literature and promotes a reading culture throughout the school.
10. Mr/Ms Fix It: Prefers being out and about, fixing things and making improvements to the school grounds; often seen in small schools with a toolbelt and a can-do attitude.

The question is, who are you? And how are you going to drive this school forward while taking the whole learning community with you?

Building trust and rapport is essential. Nobody likes a bully, a know-it-all or to be patronised or belittled. Being authentic and sharing something of your own failings and vulnerabilities helps. Your implicit message is, 'I'm not perfect, and I don't expect you to be, but I do expect teamwork, honesty, loyalty and hard work.'

One headteacher shares the tale of moving to a new school. In the first meeting, he put up his new vision statement and a list of 12 staff meetings for term 1 covering everything from child protection to assessment, curriculum and educational research, and everything in between. Needless to say, at the end of the first term, staff were bewildered and overloaded and wondering, whose school is this, anyway?

The lesson is be yourself and allow your school community to be who they are, and through constructing a rapport based on trust and mutual respect your new direction will not only be tolerated but supported.

Reflect

Part A

- What is my philosophy of education – can I sum it up in a few words? Has it changed over time?
- What are my professional strengths and weaknesses?
- When introducing yourself as a new head, what are your non-negotiables? Why choose these?
- Who are you? The perfectionist, the innovator, the team player, the leader, the communicator, the mediator, the mentor, the optimist, the pragmatist, the details person, the workaholic or the networker?

Part B

- Who do you have in your senior team?

Depending on the size of your school, this could range from two to seven people or more. The key point is that your team is comprised of complementary skills, experience and character types to ensure you are really effective as a group.

A whole brain team could have the following attributes: the visionary (usually the head), the strategist, the analyser, the organiser (usually the deputy headteacher), the connectors – cascading information, the innovator, the diplomat and the mentor.

If you know, for instance, that you have big ideas based on experience and research, but you lack the completer finisher piece, then you need to hire accordingly. That could be a great personal assistant, if budgets allow, or it could be your deputy.

It is only when you are being your authentic self that people will really trust and buy into what you are saying. It is also the state that will feel most natural to you – when you are not acting a role, you are most likely to feel comfortable and accomplished. Building a complementary team around you will ensure success as you have all bases covered when delivering school improvement.

- But who cares for the carers?

Being a headteacher can take over your whole life – and while you learn the ropes that's to be expected. However, as quickly as possible, the advice is to make sure you have personal boundaries. For instance, SLT WhatsApp groups pinging till 11pm is a bad idea (unless it's an emergency). What about email traffic over the weekends? The truth is that if the headteacher is emailing all the time, the message to everyone else is, 'you should be too!'

VARIABLE THROTTLE

There are times, of course, when you will plant your foot firmly on the accelerator to ensure that a project, school journey, child protection issue, grant application or health and safety issue is resolved as soon as possible. But when you are out of those modes, it's OK to reduce your revs and allow the team to settle and embed what you are doing. In effect, you are trying to deliver the school's goals without burning yourself or your team out.

SELF-CARE FOR HEADTEACHERS

Primary school headteachers hold a pivotal role, steering the school community with vision and determination. However, this responsibility can be all-consuming, making it essential for headteachers to prioritise

YOURSELF

their own health and wellbeing to lead effectively. Remember what they tell you on a plane: if there is an emergency, put your own oxygen mask on first before helping others. You are no good to your school if you're shattered and disillusioned at home on long-term sick.

Which self-care from the list below could help you and your team?

N.B. If you're going to hold a wellbeing workshop, don't do it late in the day when everyone is tired. Teachers often say the best wellbeing session they've had was time to sort out their classroom or go home early to be with their family.

- Physical health – Daily exercise is a must, whether it's a morning walk, yoga or a gym session. This not only boosts energy levels but also provides a crucial mental break. Nutrition is equally important; maintaining a balanced diet rich in fruit, vegetables and hydration sustains focus and resilience.

- Mental health – The demands of leadership can be overwhelming, making mental wellbeing a priority. Mindfulness practices, such as meditation or deep breathing exercises, can help manage stress and maintain clarity in decision-making. Additionally, taking regular breaks throughout the day, even for just a few minutes, can prevent burnout. It's also crucial to set boundaries, ensuring work doesn't encroach on personal time, which allows for proper rest and recovery. Getting to the toilet can be a challenge some days – sometimes people will just have to wait for you.

- Emotional wellbeing – Building a strong support network, both professionally and personally, is vital. Sharing challenges with peers or seeking mentorship can provide new perspectives and reduce feelings of isolation. Remembering to celebrate small victories and practising gratitude can shift the focus from the pressures to the positive aspects of the role.

- Social health – Connection is key. Maintaining relationships with colleagues, friends and family outside of school fosters a sense of belonging and support. Regularly engaging in hobbies or activities that bring joy can also rejuvenate the spirit and maintain a balanced life.

ASIDE

By prioritising aspects of health and wellbeing, headteachers not only enhance their own quality of life but also set a powerful example for their school community, leading with both wisdom and vitality.

Sometimes, it's helpful to look at the 'wheel of life' (see Figure 6) — commonly used by life coaches. It might highlight areas that are out of balance in your life — give it a go!

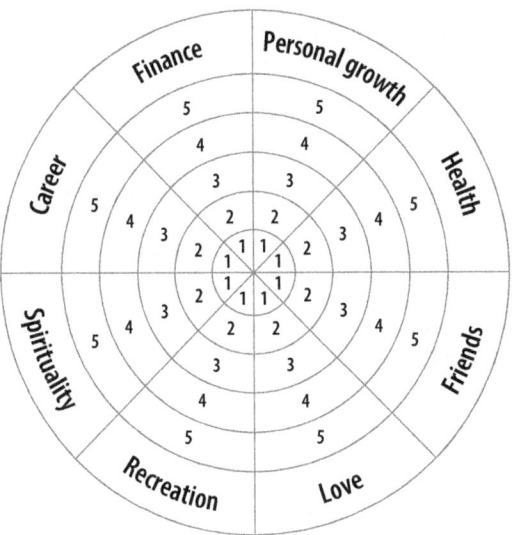

Figure 6. The wheel of life

Source: Mindful Coaching Tools

ZILLIONS

> No matter what people tell you, words and ideas can change the world.
>
> *Dead Poets Society* (1989)

Being a primary school headteacher is a journey unlike any other. It requires that you have zillions of ideas. From activities and events, to trips and visitors, to PTA events and staff training, and know how to fit all of this into a tight budget.

It is a role steeped in joy, laden with challenges and brimming with the immense privilege of shaping young minds. On a good day it is an adventure filled with opportunities to inspire, guide and nurture the next generation. On a bad day it can be soul-destroying, as it's on you personally to make the many moving parts synchronise and mesh seamlessly. Having a good team around you is essential: a multifaceted team with complementary skills and experiences who are hard-working and loyal to the cause – that cocktail will ensure success.

THE JOYS

One of the greatest joys of being a primary school headteacher is witnessing the spark of curiosity in children's eyes. From their first day in reception to their final day in Year 6, watching children grow and develop is incredibly rewarding. Each milestone they achieve, whether it's learning to read, mastering multiplication or confidently presenting a project in assembly, is a testament to the collective efforts of teachers, parents and you the headteacher.

The relationships built with students are another source of immense joy. Knowing each child by name, understanding their strengths and weaknesses, and seeing them flourish under your guidance is a daily reminder of the impact you have. These connections often extend beyond the classroom, as you celebrate their successes and support them through their challenges.

Relationships with parents can be difficult at times, and it can feel like an uneven playing field when the WhatsApp groups light up with gossip and misinformation, while you must only communicate in an informed and professional manner. Over time, though, parents will see that you are someone to trust, someone to give time to and someone whose mission is clearly dedicated to helping the children learn.

Creating a positive school culture is also a joyful endeavour. As a headteacher, you have the opportunity to foster an environment where kindness, respect and inclusivity are the norms. Seeing students collaborate, support each other and demonstrate empathy fills you with pride and reinforces the importance of your role. 'Achieving together' moving from the reception display into classrooms, corridors and the sports field.

Moreover, the opportunity to innovate in education is exhilarating. Implementing new teaching methods, integrating technology and developing creative curriculums allows you to keep the learning fresh and exciting – seeing innovations like AI in education as the next opportunity in the long history of educational reform and improvements.

The satisfaction of seeing these innovations lead to improved student engagement and achievement is unparalleled, and don't be afraid of the odd tear or two. Those are the tears of pride, relief that it worked and joy for a school really serving its community to the full.

THE CHALLENGES

Headship is not without its challenges. One of the most significant is balancing administrative duties with the need to be present and engaged with students and staff. Try not to get barricaded in your office all day with meetings, phone calls and emails – try to be visible and present for the children and staff.

The myriad of responsibilities, from managing budgets to ensuring compliance with regulations, can be overwhelming. It requires a delicate balance to ensure that these tasks do not overshadow the core mission of education.

Dealing with diverse needs is another challenge. Each child is unique, with different backgrounds, abilities and learning styles. Ensuring that every student receives the support they need to succeed requires a deep understanding of inclusive education practices and the ability to adapt strategies to meet individual needs.

Further, have the tenacity to ask for more funding for your SEND students, for example, and push back when you feel the latest requirement could capsize your school. You are responsible for the pupils' achievement in the school – but also for staff wellbeing. Therefore, you must make informed choices about which initiatives to go with, which to dodge and when enough is enough for your team.

Navigating the complexities of staff management is challenging. Supporting teachers, addressing their concerns and fostering professional development are critical to creating a positive working environment. However, managing conflicts, ensuring staff wellbeing and maintaining high standards can be demanding.

How do you and your SLT currently manage difficult conversations with staff?

- Do you have a school approach which includes support plans, template letters, guidance information for line managers and teachers, and formal HR policies and processes in place?
- What effect does poor performance that goes unchallenged have on top-performing teachers?

The pressure to meet external expectations, such as standardised test scores and inspection outcomes, can be intense. While these measures are important, they can sometimes overshadow the holistic development of students. Striking a balance between achieving academic excellence and nurturing well-rounded individuals is a constant challenge.

The headteacher must set the tone for the ethos of the school in assemblies, staff meetings and parents' meetings, noticing the achievements of the whole learning community and heaping praise on those who have made great efforts, not just those who have won or scored the highest marks.

THE PRIVILEGE

Despite the challenges, the role of a primary school headteacher is a profound privilege. The opportunity to shape young minds and influence their futures is a responsibility that carries immense weight and significance. Every decision made, every policy implemented and every interaction with students has the potential to leave a lasting impact. The best ensure this is a profoundly positive impact which reverberates for a lifetime.

Being a headteacher allows you to be a role model. Your actions, attitudes and values set the tone for the entire school community. Demonstrating qualities such as integrity, resilience and compassion not only inspires students but also instils these values in them. (See the Nolan Principles – the seven principles of public life: Committee on Standards in Public Life, 1995).

The privilege of being entrusted with the education and wellbeing of children is immense. Parents place their trust in you to provide a safe, nurturing and stimulating environment for their children.

One international principal tells the story of running a British school in the UAE. When meeting a local parent about some bad behaviour, the parent responded, 'He is your son, mister – we trust you to do what is best.' This trust is a powerful motivator to continually strive for excellence and ensure that every child receives the best possible education.

Having the platform to advocate for children and influence educational policy is another significant privilege. Whether it is working with local authorities, participating in professional networks or contributing to national discussions, headteachers have the opportunity to shape the broader educational landscape.

How could your voice add to the educational debate locally and nationally?

Could your team write a short case study about a success you have had recently? Could you network more effectively with other schools in similar circumstances to share ideas, resources and initiatives?

One of the most fulfilling aspects of being a headteacher is the opportunity to motivate, encourage and direct youngsters towards becoming the best versions of themselves.

STAY CURRENT

My advice to you, mighty leader, is to stay up to date with the latest in educational research, thinking, approaches and technologies. Some do this through reading, listening to podcasts, attending meetings and developing their training and qualification – for example, a master's in educational leadership, National Professional Qualification for Headship or Executive Leadership, or even Doctor of Education (EdD) or Doctor of Philosophy (PhD) in education. (Who has the time, you ask? Those who make time is the glib answer.)

TAKE CARE, SERIOUSLY

Who looks after the caregivers? Who supports those supporting everyone else? It's true that leadership can be lonely at times, but successful leaders manage to find a way to cope and even thrive. Strategies include proper delegation across the school, supervision to ensure all feel supported, strong honest relationships that can stand feedback when things start to wobble, and a chair of governors who will listen and support when needed.

But most of all you need family and friends to whom you can talk to decompress, distract you and give you perspective on your job. That's right, it's just a job after all. (Probably one of the most impactful jobs as all layers of society travel through our schools, but still a job.)

Ensure your mobile phone is not the most important 'person' at home, on holiday or when you are taking your children out for the day. Creating healthy boundaries around checking emails at home will lessen your family feeling like they never have your full attention.

You are the captain of the ship – set the direction and brief the crew. There will be storms ahead, but together you will overcome any obstacle and go on an amazing journey.

ASIDE

'O Captain! My Captain!' by Walt Whitman (1819-1892) mourns the loss of a revered leader (Abraham Lincoln) just as they reach the triumphant end of a perilous journey, the American Civil War. It's a poignant mix of celebration and sorrow.

Oh Captain! My Captain.

O Captain! my Captain! our fearful trip is done,

The ship has weather'd every rack, the prize we sought is won,

The port is near, the bells I hear, the people all exulting,

While follow eyes the steady keel, the vessel grim and daring;

(Whitman, 1892)

***

O Me! O Life!

O Me! O life! of the questions of these recurring, . . .

The question, O me! so sad, recurring—What good amid these, O me, O life?

Answer.

That you are here—that life exists and identity,

That the powerful play goes on, and you may contribute a verse.

(Whitman, 1892)

What will your verse be? (If you have not seen the 1989 film *Dead Poets Society* – then that is your homework!)

SECTION TWO

THE FIVE KEYS TO A SUCCESSFUL SCHOOL

Chris Nourse-Grewal

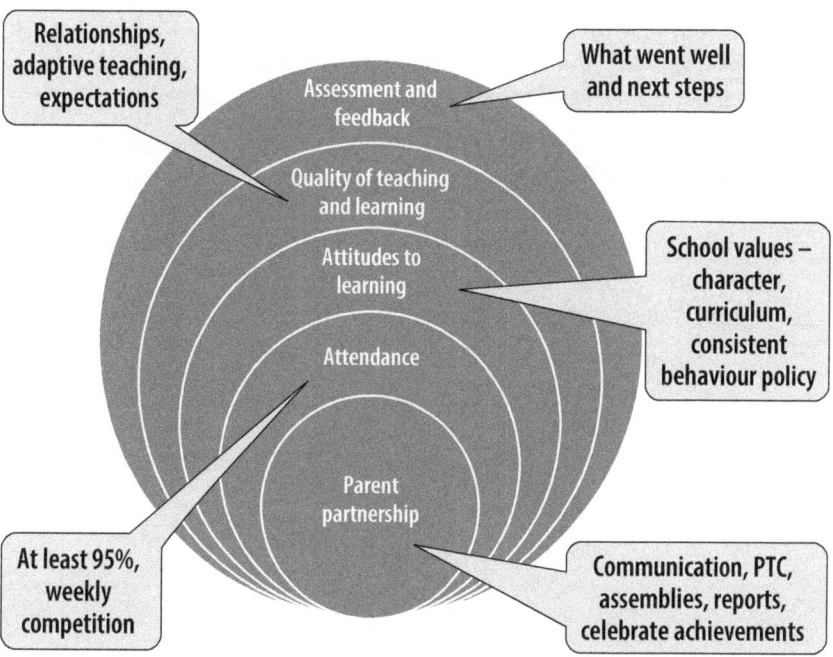

1. Parents understand the importance of their children attending school regularly and wish to be in a meaningful partnership with the school.
2. Children attend school at least 95% of the time. (Evidence suggests that students with the highest attendance achieve the highest grades.)

3. The school has clear expectations for behaviour based on values, and attitudes and behaviours for learning are taught and modelled. Pupil voice also supports the ongoing school improvement agenda. Learners thrive in a positive environment with a rich mix of activities and learning experiences. Pupil wellbeing is constantly considered, and teachers, counsellors, teaching assistants and senior staff work collaboratively to safeguard and support young people. Personal goals are set termly, and older students research and evaluate their future plans – university and further education options are starting to be considered.
4. Teachers are selected carefully and once inducted have a clear growth plan to constantly improve (Teachers' Standards). Lesson observations, book looks and pupil progress data support both teacher appraisal and professional development needs.
5. Internal assessments are standards based and moderated to be at year-level expectations and beyond – leading to closer alignment to national and international benchmarks. Students with additional needs have adapted assessments to showcase their progress (learning pathways). Teacher feedback both celebrates pupils' successes and signposts their next steps in learning.

TEACHING AND LEARNING CONTINUA

Gareth Coombes

Continua is a comprehensive, developmental resource that supports leaders and teachers in evaluating the impact of teaching in their schools. It provides four progressive descriptors of improving performance that enable clarity and consistency within the school, for leaders and teachers. These are based on Ofsted's 'unsatisfactory', 'improving but in need of improvement', 'good' and 'outstanding'.

The content of Continua is based on extensive research, of which the greatest influences have been the work of the Education Endowment Foundation, John Hattie and the Hay McBer research into teacher effectiveness. The use of Continua enables leaders to have an overview of both the collective and the individual practice of teachers in the school. This enables a more effective identification of consistent strengths and whole-school and individual development needs. It also identifies who may be able to support development through sharing expertise.

Source: Gareth Coombes, The Teaching and Learning Continua

THE KBZA CHARACTER CURRICULUM

At KBZA school, we use this table of definitions to help us both monitor individual students' character for learning scores and then target groups of students for support in lessons, mentorship or team around the child discussions.

Student's character for learning score

\multicolumn{3}{c	}{Student's Character for Learning (CfL) score}
CfL score	Category	Description
1	Outstanding learner	The student engages fully in lessons, taking every opportunity to extend understanding through questions – evidence seen in books/work produced.
		The student has impeccable time-keeping, attendance, uniform and equipment standards.
		The student leads the learning in the classroom.
		The student seeks challenge and independently extends their learning outside of the classroom. The student is going above and beyond in all aspects of learning.
		Character focus is clearly being demonstrated in all aspects of behaviour.

	Student's Character for Learning (CfL) score	
CfL score	**Category**	**Description**
2	Ambitious learner	The student is always fully engaged in all lessons and actively always listens.
		The student has excellent time-keeping, attendance, uniform and equipment standards.
		The student is always focused in lessons and completes all their work to an exceptional standard.
		The student is always looking how to improve their work, listens to the teacher's feedback and applies improvements independently and to a high standard.
		The student always has a positive attitude in lessons and is determined to try the most challenging tasks.
		The student has a positive influence on the learning of others, engages in discussions, showing empathy to others and always adhering to the school expectations.
		Character focus is being demonstrated in all aspects of behaviour.
3	Engaged learner	The student is engaged in most of the lesson and actively listens consistently.
		The student often has very good time-keeping, attendance, uniform and equipment standards.
		The student is focused in lessons and completes their work to a good standard most of the time.
		The student is willing to improve their work, and listens to teachers' feedback and makes improvements when prompted.
		The student usually has a positive attitude in lessons and is determined even when tasks get challenging.
		The student is enthusiastic most of the time, is engaged in discussions and can show empathy to others.
		The student tries to adhere to the school expectations and responds quickly if not.
		Character focus is often demonstrated in aspects of behaviour.

THE KBZA CHARACTER CURRICULUM

	Student's Character for Learning (CfL) score	
CfL score	Category	Description
4	Passive learner	The student is sometimes disengaged in lessons but does try to listen.
		The student sometimes has good time-keeping, attendance, uniform and equipment standards but may need prompting regularly on these.
		The student can focus on lessons, but this isn't always to the best standard.
		When prompted by the teacher, the student wants to improve their work, and responds to feedback, but this may not be in as much detail based on their capability. The student sometimes gives up when tasks get hard or they get stuck. They can sometimes show a lack of effort.
		Character focus is sometimes demonstrated in aspects of behaviour.
5	Reluctant learner	The student is regularly disengaged and does not always try to listen during class discussion.
		The student rarely has good time-keeping, attendance, uniform and equipment standards and will regularly need prompting on these.
		The student does not focus on lessons and is often off task or produces work of an unsatisfactory standard.
		The teacher must continuously prompt the student to improve their work, but the student does not always respond to feedback or easily gives up.
		The student often gives up if they find a task hard/challenging. They deliberately show a lack of effort.
		The student regularly has a negative impact on the learning of others as they don't adhere to the school expectations.
		Character focus is rarely demonstrated in aspects of behaviour.
6	Unavailable	The teacher is unable to provide a Character for Learning grade now due to one of the following factors: pupil behaviour, pupil absence, staff absence, recent change in class.

Source: Khalifa Bin Zayed Al Awal School

IN-CLASS BEHAVIOUR FLOW CHART FOR STUDENTS

This simple class behaviour flow chart can be displayed in every classroom and serves as a reminder to both teachers and learners as to what to expect if behaviour does not meet our expectations. The key of course is to consistently apply the rewards and sanctions – otherwise it can quickly fade into the wall paper.

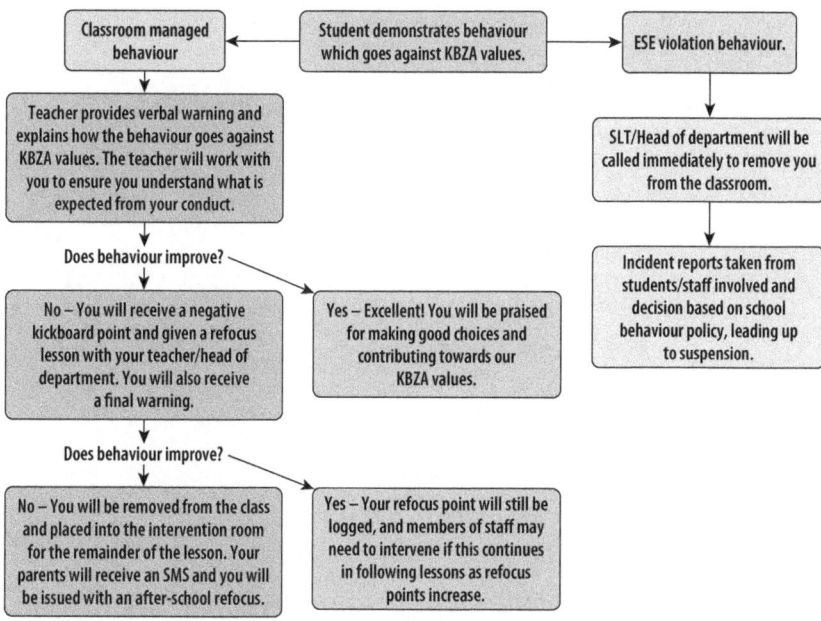

Classroom-managed – Excessive talking, dress code, tardiness, low-level disruption, drinking/eating, misuse of devices, low-level inappropriate behaviour towards peers, etc.

Immediate support – Extreme insubordination, fighting, illicit substances, serious bullying, verbal/physical intimidation, harassment, threats, etc.

Source: Khalifa Bin Zayed Al Awal School

ORACY – WHY?

Schools have become increasingly aware of the need to explicitly teach vocabulary in recent years. Having poor language at a young age can lead to reading difficulties in adulthood and a high chance of unemployment. Pupils facing disadvantage are likely to be disproportionately affected.

The Curriculum with Unity Schools Partnership (CUSP) has a mental model which aims to move language from superficial receptive stores to embedded expressive stores. Pupils should read, see and hear target language, with teachers giving concise definitions. As the target language is used in multiple contexts to build schemes around new words, helping them build connections so that the language can be used in tasks and eventually across subject disciplines.

The website for the Curriculum with Unity Schools Partnership (CUSP) has some useful resources: https://www.unity-curriculum.co.uk.

MIDDLE LEADERS – PUPIL PROGRESS PROFORMA

Here are some prompts that may guide you when you meet your middle leaders for line management conversations about attainment and progress of pupils.

Term 1 pupil progress meeting

Year:

Teacher:

1. External data

External data headlines	
CAT 4 Average (ARE)	SAS
NGRT Average (ARE)	SAS

2. Internal data analysis

English	
What percentage of students are currently at age-related expectation?	
Are there any students whose data you are positively surprised about (why might this be)?	
Are there any students whose data you are concerned about (how can we support them further)?	
Any KPI trends (female, male, SEND, homegrown students, etc.)?	
AOB:	

Maths	
What percentage of students are currently at age-related expectation?	
Are there any students whose data you are positively surprised about (why might this be)?	
Are there any students whose data you are concerned about (how can we support them further)?	
Any KPI trends (female, male, SEND, homegrown students, etc.)?	
AOB:	

Science	
What percentage of students are currently at age-related expectation?	
Are there any students whose data you are positively surprised about (why might this be)?	
Are there any students whose data you are concerned about (how can we support them further)?	
Any KPI trends (female, male, SEND, homegrown students, etc.)?	
AOB:	

3. Questions for teachers/heads of department

T1 data drop considerations:

- Analyse data to identify gaps and trends: Review assessment results to pinpoint specific areas of strength and weakness for both individuals and groups, aligning findings with curriculum objectives.
- Implement DIRT (dedicated improvement and reflection time): Allocate time for students to reflect on feedback, correct mistakes, and act on specific improvement targets to consolidate their learning and foster metacognition.

- Adjust planning and teaching: Use assessment data to adapt schemes of work, ensuring future lessons address identified gaps and reinforce key concepts, following the principles of responsive teaching.
- Provide constructive feedback: Deliver clear, actionable feedback to students, focusing on how they can improve rather than just what they got wrong, as effective feedback is shown to have a significant impact on learning.
- Engage students in peer- and self-assessment: Encourage students to evaluate their work and that of peers to deepen understanding, develop critical thinking skills and take ownership of their learning.

Heads of department post-T1 data drop considerations:
- How can we effectively use regular, announced lesson drop-ins to support professional growth and ensure consistent teaching quality? (Highlights the importance of formative observations to foster continuous improvement and align teaching practices with departmental goals.)
- What opportunities exist for sharing best practices within the department, and how can we create a culture of collaboration and mutual learning? (Emphasise the importance of collaborative professionalism to drive teacher efficacy and student outcomes.)
- What does regular book scrutiny reveal about the quality of student work, feedback and teacher expectations, and how can this be used to improve consistency and rigour? (Suggests that reviewing student work provides valuable insights into teaching quality and curriculum implementation.)
- How are we identifying and supporting students in focus or Wave 3 students based on data, and are tailored provisions effectively meeting their needs? (Underline the role of data-driven interventions to personalise learning and improve outcomes for struggling students.)
- Are our staff inspired and motivated, and does the department foster a culture of high performance and shared accountability? (Identify inspirational leadership and a focus on high expectations

as critical factors in creating a culture of excellence and continuous improvement.)
- Check with staff whether they are using subscriptions effectively.
- For C1, are we implementing the Primary Years Programme consistently within lessons?

HOLISTIC DEVELOPMENT – BALANCING THE WHOLE CHILD

Holistic development is an approach to education that views a child's overall advancement as the outcome of everyday habits and consistently practised skills.

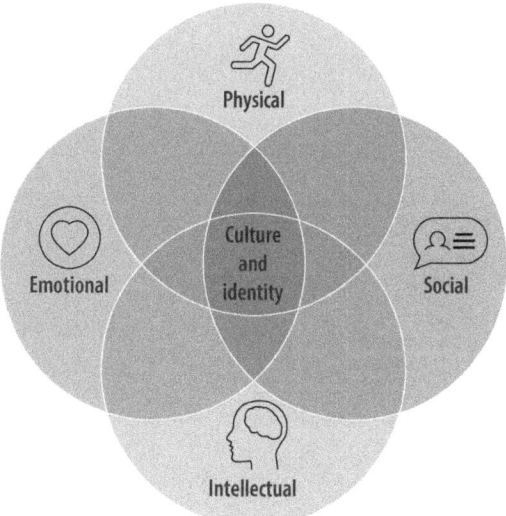

Source: Khalifa Bin Zayed Al Awal School

AI POLICY POINTS FOR GOVERNANCE

ETHICAL AND RESPONSIBLE USE OF GENERATIVE AI AND DATA TECHNOLOGIES

All users of generative AI (GenAI) and data technologies in our school, including students, teachers and administrators, are expected to use these technologies in a responsible and ethical manner. This includes respecting others, including their intellectual property rights, and avoiding any actions that could lead to negative outcomes. Further, users must adhere to all relevant laws, regulations and school policies. Users must be aware of any potential biases in these technologies and take steps to mitigate them.

Users are responsible for monitoring the results produced by GenAI systems. This includes confirming the information provided by GenAI is accurate and reliable, and reporting any concerns or issues of any GenAI output to the appropriate person or department.

GOVERNANCE AND ACCOUNTABILITY

The executive leadership team holds overall responsibility for the AI policy, delegating the implementation and oversight to the SLT, ensuring that practices are fully embedded, monitored and reported back. The AI Ethics and Safety Committee, comprising the dean of the school, the head of health, pastoral and wellbeing, the IT officer and the respective head of cycle, is tasked with overseeing adherence to ethical standards and safety protocols. All members of the KBZA school community are informed of the individuals holding these roles. The AI Ethics and Safety Committee is responsible for staying informed about current developments and guidance from relevant bodies such as the Ministry of Education UAE.

THE RIPPLE EFFECT

Building a values-based culture through authentic relationships and high expectations can give students a sense of belonging and identity, which drives their intrinsic motivation to strive for personal and academic growth.

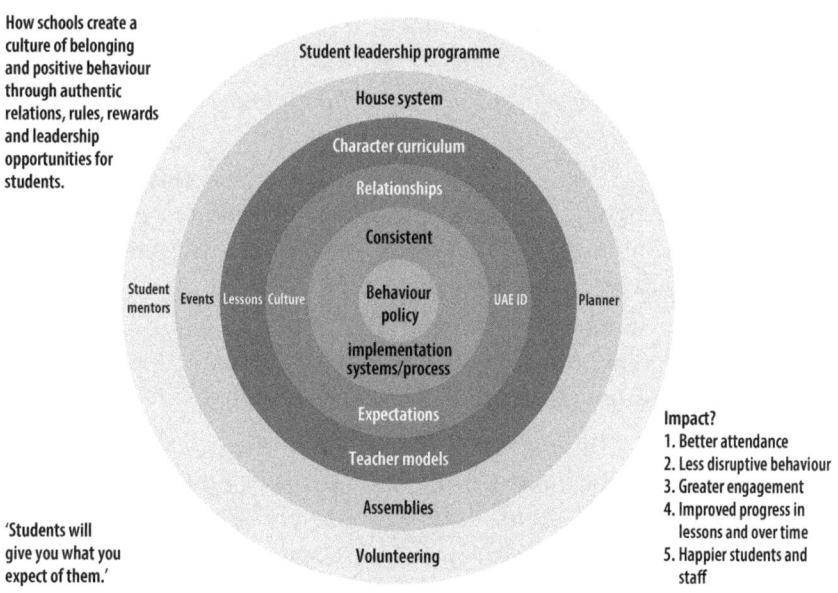

Source: Khalifa Bin Zayed Al Awal School

REFERENCES

Avgerinou, V. (2019). Do teaching assistants improve pupil outcomes in mainstream schools? *Chartered College Research Hub.* https://my.chartered.college/research-hub/do-teaching-assistants-improve-pupil-outcomes-in-mainstream-schools

BBC. (2021). Ian Wright's teacher gave him direction and purpose during his turbulent upbringing [Video]. *YouTube.* https://www.youtube.com/watch?v=6caCqn_nD6o

BBC News. (2016, 9 May). Sats tests letter to pupils goes viral. https://www.bbc.co.uk/news/uk-england-36247429

Bosanquet, P., Radford, J., & Webster, R. (2016). *The teaching assistant's guide to effective interaction: How to maximise your practice.* Routledge.

Branson, R. (2015). *The Virgin way: Everything I know about leadership.* Portfolio.

Burnett, C. (2017, 9 October). 7 touching books to help kids understand death and grief [Blog]. *Scholastic.* https://www.scholastic.com/parents/books-and-reading/raise-a-reader-blog/7-touching-books-to-help-kids-understand-death-and-grief.html

Committee on Standards in Public Life. (1995, 31 May). The Seven Principles of Public Life. https://www.gov.uk/government/publications/the-7-principles-of-public-life/the-7-principles-of-public-life--2

Coombes, Gareth. https://www.teachingcontinua.com

Department for Education. (2010). *The Importance of Teaching: The Schools White Paper 2010.* https://assets.publishing.service.gov.uk/media/5a7b4029ed915d3ed9063285/CM-7980.pdf

Department for Education. (2011). *Teachers' Standards: Guidance for school leaders, school staff and governing bodies* (updated June 2013 and December 2021). https://www.gov.uk/government/publications/teachers-standards

Department for Education. (2023, 18 May). Why is school attendance so important and what are the risks of missing a day? [Blog]. https://educationhub.blog.gov.uk/2023/05/school-attendance-important-risks-missing-day

Department for Education. (2025, 25 March). Pupil premium: overview. https://www.gov.uk/government/publications/pupil-premium/pupil-premium

Education Endowment Foundation. (n.d.). A school's guide to implementation: Implementation process. https://d2tic4wvo1iusb.cloudfront.net/production/eef-guidance-reports/implementation/implementation_process_graphic.pdf?v=1723181630

Education Endowment Foundation. (2021). Performance pay. https://educationendowmentfoundation.org.uk/education-evidence/teaching-learning-toolkit/performance-pay

Education Endowment Foundation. (2024). *The EEF guide to the pupil premium.* https://educationendowmentfoundation.org.uk/education-evidence/using-pupil-premium

Egan, G. (2017). *The skilled helper: A client-centred approach* (2nd EMEA ed.). Cengage Learning EMEA.

Ellis, S., & Tod, J. (2018). *Behaviour for learning: Promoting positive relationships in the classroom.* Routledge.

Hattie, J. (2008). *Visible learning: A synthesis of over 800 meta-analyses relating to achievement.* Routledge.

International Baccalaureate. (2023, 1 March). Statement from the IB about ChatGPT and artificial intelligence in assessment and education. https://www.ibo.org/news/news-about-the-ib/statement-from-the-ib-about-chatgpt-and-artificial-intelligence-in-assessment-and-education

Jubilee Centre for Character & Virtues. (n.d.). Key stage 2 parent resources. https://www.jubileecentre.ac.uk/character-education-/key-stage-2-parent-resources

Khan, S. (2024). *Brave new words: How AI will revolutionize education (and why that's a good thing).* Penguin Random House.

Khalifa Bin Zayed Al Awal School. https://www.kbza.sch.ae

Kipling, R. (1902). *The Elephant's Child.* In *Just So Stories.* Macmillan.

Kipling, R. (1919). 'My Boy Jack'. In *The Years Between*. Macmillan.

Kubrick, S. (Director). (1968). *2001: A Space Odyssey* [Film]. Metro-Goldwyn-Mayer.

Maguire, E. A., Gadian, D. G., Johnsrude, I. S., Good, C. D., Ashburner, J., Frackowiak, R. S. J., & Frith, C. D. (2000). Navigation-related structural change in the hippocampi of taxi drivers. *Proceedings of the National Academy of Sciences, 97*(8), 4398–4403. https://doi.org/10.1073/pnas.070039597

Michigan Department of Education. (n.d.). *Whole child definition*. https://www.michigan.gov/mde/resources/michigans-top-10-strategic-education-plan/definitions/whole-child

Mindful Coaching Tools. https://www.mindfulcoachingtools.com/

Montessori, M. (1988). *The discovery of the child*. Random House.

NAHT. (2024a). Responding to Ofsted's 'Big Listen' – guidance for members. https://www.naht.org.uk/About-Us/NAHT-Crown-Dependencies/ArtMID/1090/ArticleID/2379/Responding-to-Ofsted's-'Big-Listen'-guidance-for-members

NAHT. (2024b). *Rethinking school inspection: Delivering fair, proportionate, and humane school accountability*. https://www.naht.org.uk/Portals/0/PDF%27s/Reports/NAHT-Ofsted-report_Jan_2024_FINAL_REPORT_.pdf?ver=2024-01-16-172409-693

NASUWT. (n.d.). Performance management – a practical guide (England). https://www.nasuwt.org.uk/advice/performance-management/performance-management-a-practical-guide-england.html

Ofsted. (2011). *Supporting children with challenging behaviour through a nurture group approach*. https://assets.publishing.service.gov.uk/media/5a800636e5274a2e8ab4dbb5/Supporting_children_with_challenging_behaviour_through_a_nurture_group_approach.pdf

Ofsted. (2024, 16 September). *School inspection handbook*. https://www.gov.uk/government/publications/school-inspection-handbook-eif/school-inspection-handbook-for-september-2023

Oliver, J. (Presenter). (2005). *Jamie's school dinners* [TV series]. Channel 4.

Peter, L. J., & Hull, R. (1994). *The Peter principle: Why things always go wrong*. Souvenir Press.

raisingchildren.net.au. (2025). Self-regulation: children and teenagers. Suitable for 1–18 years. https://raisingchildren.net.au/toddlers/behaviour/understanding-behaviour/self-regulation

Rogers, C. (1951). *Client-centered therapy: Its current practice, implications and theory.* Constable.

Royal College of Paediatrics and Child Health. (2020). Child poverty. https://stateofchildhealth.rcpch.ac.uk/evidence/family-and-social-environment/child-poverty

Seldon, A. (2017). *The fourth education revolution: Will artificial intelligence liberate or infantilise humanity?* University of Buckingham Press.

Sinek, S. (2014). *Leaders eat last: Why some teams pull together and others don't.* Portfolio/Penguin.

Stewart, R., & Campbell, A. (Hosts). (2021–present). *The rest is politics* [Podcast]. Goalhanger.

Taylor, M. (2005, 18 October). 'His input can be seen everywhere'. *The Guardian.* https://www.theguardian.com/education/2005/oct/18/teachingawards2006.teachingawards7

Teacher Workload Advisory Group. (2018). *Making data work: Report of the Teacher Workload Advisory Group.* https://www.gov.uk/government/publications/teacher-workload-advisory-group-report-and-government-response

Teachmate. (n.d.). Instant support for teachers. Heavy lifting by AI. https://teachmateai.com/?gad_source=1&gbraid=0AAAAA9pu7WX9lZ-KeKTBF83ZReJhigB74&gclid=EAIaIQobChMI2_KckqGkiAMV8FtBAh2yKCpREAAYASAAEgI7YfD_BwE

UCL Institute of Education. (2020, 24 November). Research shows 'a sense of belonging' is important for pupils' learning and behaviour. https://www.ucl.ac.uk/ioe/news/2020/nov/research-shows-sense-belonging-important-pupils-learning-and-behaviour

Unity Schools Partnership. (n.d.). Curriculum with Unity Schools Partnership (CUSP). https://www.unity-curriculum.co.uk

Webster, R., & Blatchford, P. (2013). *Making a statement: A study of the experiences of pupils with SEN and the use of teaching assistants in mainstream primary schools.* Institute of Education, University of London.

Webster, R., & Blatchford, P. (2015). *Maximising the impact of teaching assistants: Guidance for school leaders and teachers.* Routledge.

Weir, P. (Director). (1989). *Dead Poets Society* [Film]. Touchstone Pictures.

Whitman, W. (1892). *Leaves of grass. The deathbed edition.* David McKay.

Worden, J. W. (2009). *Grief counseling and grief therapy: A handbook for the mental health practitioner* (4th ed.). Springer.

Xinyue. (2023, 19 September). The fascinating intersection of piano and neuroscience. *London Piano Institute.* https://www.londonpianoinstitute.co.uk/fascinating-intersection-of-piano-and-neuroscience

The A–Z series focuses on the 'fun and fundamentals' of what's happening in primary, special and secondary schools today. Each title is written by a leading practitioner, adopting a series approach of reflection, advice and provocation.

As a group of authors with a strong belief in the power of education to shape and change young people's lives, we hope teachers and leaders in the UK and internationally enjoy what we have to say.

Roy Blatchford, series editor

The A–Z of Great Classrooms (2023)

The A–Z of Secondary Leadership (2023)

The A–Z of Primary Maths (2024)

The A–Z of School Improvement (2024)

The A–Z of Diversity and Inclusion (2024)

The A–Z of Trust Leadership (2024)

The A–Z of International School Leadership (2024)

The A–Z of Special Educational Needs (2024)

The A–Z of Early Career Teaching (2024)

The A–Z of Student Wellbeing (2025)

The A–Z of Addressing Disadvantage (2025)

The A–Z of Independent School Leadership (2025)

The A–Z of Primary English (2025)

The A–Z of Good Governance (forthcoming)

The A–Z of Primary Leadership (forthcoming)

Personalised professional development from Hachette Learning Academy

A simple way to boost career progression, staff motivation and educational excellence.

Our online courses are:

 Aligned with **teaching competency frameworks**

 Written by experts in education, including Hachette Learning authors (formerly John Catt)

 Created to enable educators to **develop competencies** linked to their professional development aspirations

 Powered by adaptive learning, to accommodate a diverse range of skills, knowledge and understanding

 Designed to support **effective learning and high-impact teaching**

www.hachettelearning.com/academy